LEADING THE CHARGE FOR CHANGE

Women Inspiring Leadership

DR. JOLENE CHURCH & DR. ENNETTE MORTON

DEDICATION

To the pillars of strength and light in my life:

To my grandmother, whose audacity, conviction, and resilience remain an eternal beacon for me.

To my mother, whose tireless work ethic is not just something I admire, but a legacy I strive to uphold.

To Ennette, my mentor and co-author, who saw in me the potential I was yet to recognize and ignited the flame of scholarly pursuit.

And to Steve "Hawsie", my anchor and compass, whose unwavering support and love fortify me every single day.

Thank you, my cherished village, for sculpting me into the change-maker and indomitable leader I have become. Your imprints are etched deeply in every step I take.

With endless gratitude and love,

Jolene Church

DEDICATION

To my unwavering sources of inspiration:

First, glory be to God through which all things are possible.

To my mom and dad for instilling the love of learning, importance of education and are my lifelong role models. This book carries a piece of your spirit within its pages.

To my daughter Ashley, my precious baby girl, you are a constant source of love, joy, and you give my life purpose.

To James, my wonderful husband, thank you for your unconditional love, support, and steadfast belief in me.

And to Jolene, my co-author and dear colleague, thank you for guiding us through the twists and turns of this project. Your boundless patience and encouragement have propelled me to new heights in my writing journey.

To my sister Dee, you are my little angel.

Forever grateful and thankful,

Ennette Morton

TABLE OF CONTENTS

Foreword 1

Introduction 9

Chapter 1.. 19
Historical Context of Women in Leadership

Chapter 2.. 37
Empowering Mindsets for Female Leaders

Chapter 3.. 61
Powerful Communication: Finding Your Voice

Chapter 4.. 85
The Power of the Network

Chapter 5.. 105
Work-Life Balance and Self-Care as Role Models for the Next Generation

Chapter 6.. 127
Leadership Styles and Strategies

Chapter 7.. 151
Creating an Inclusive and Diverse Work Environment

Chapter 8.. 175
Nurturing Future Female Leaders

Chapter 9.. 195
Women in Historical Male-Dominated Fields

Chapter 10... 215
The Journey Towards A Beautiful Future

About the Authors 283
Dr. Jolene Church
Dr. Ennette Morton

Bibliography 287

FOREWORD

I'm thrilled that you've chosen to pick up this wonderful read and to embark on a journey with these two fantastic author-leaders, Dr. Jolene Church and Dr. Ennette Morton. I was immediately pulled into the stories of the women they chose to highlight, and, believe me, you will too.

I love a good read where you can cozy up with a cup of tea or coffee or a glass of wine, and you find yourself exclaiming out loud over a part that catches you off guard. I did that so many times reading this delight of a book that I lost count.

I wasn't expecting the raw stories of Stacy Shewey or Kathleen Hostert to choke me up. And then to get to Chapter 10 only to find myself laughing and nodding at the notion of accepting myself, flaws and all. It's taken me a long time to get there, but thankfully you can jumpstart your journey to self-acceptance, or help a younger woman get there faster, by reading this gem of a book. I'm not going to ruin the surprise of the many gloriously unique stories woven into this singular book by even hinting further. You'll find absolute gold in this finely written book and enjoy the stories as you come across them.

I challenge you to recognize this as an essential guidebook for women who feel maybe just a twinge or an inclination, let alone compelled, to inspire and mentor the future generation of female leaders but are unsure where to start or whether they are the right fit for the task. It is more crucial than ever to empower young girls to be bold, confident, and unafraid to take on leadership roles and create meaningful change. Personally, it took me a while to get to that point in my own life. I believe if I'd had this wonderful resource to read when I was growing up, I would have been a better mentor and a more confident example for other women. Less focused on me, more focused on us.

While I was definitely an achievement oriented woman growing up, it was more in reaction to the mixed messages I had coming at me non-stop. I had the classic, 'be a nice good girl, and don't make a scene' ingrained in me. Yet I also felt an enormous pressure of a small town girl from rural Canada who needed to break free perched almost tangibly on my shoulders, weighing me down.

With these two conflicting messages gnawing at me, I hurdled my way through an undergraduate in political studies, spent a semester in Japan, charged off to law school, took a leave of absence to spend a year living abroad in Europe, went back to law school but spent a semester of taking international law in Japan, created my own unique law practice 'pet and animal law' including setting legal precedents in completely unchartered territory gaining me (and my dog) lots of talk show and other earned media time, moved to California, and, became the became the Chief of Staff to the Mayor of the City of Riverside, California by age 30. And those are just the basic highlights. Whew, I was living the dream.

Only it wasn't my dream. It was some societally ingrained dream that I'd absorbed into my very being, telling me what success for a small town girl, who'd escaped sure boredom and monotony, should look like.

You can only imagine how many times I looked around a large boardroom table and was the only

woman at the table. One might say I had it coming since I'd chosen law and politics to make my mark. You might be surprised at how many times I had to muster my inner strength to be sure to use power postures, speak up and verbalize clearly and concisely, aka be loud, (because a soft spoken woman at a business boardroom…well, that just wouldn't do), and choose my opportunities to contribute only when I knew I had something pretty much earth shattering to share. These are not the kinds of problems women should have to think about when they go into a business meeting or a community meeting.

And certainly not if they've managed to take the gigantic leap into running for political office. And yet, these are the worries that persist and plague us, and why this book is ever so important.

Still, the first stages of my journey, which only got busier with each passing year, were so focused on accomplishments that I didn't really create meaningful change. I didn't spend a lot of time mentoring others. I just got busier, and busier…and then just a bit busier. Without the benefit of guideposts, such as "Leading the Charge for Change" provides, especially the sections in each chapter giving concrete actions and the Key Takeaways, I simply charged onward like a bull with a red flag in front of its face.

Enter stage left, the idea to write a book to tackle head on the myth of nice guys and gals finish last. I knew intuitively that this had to be a myth, and I set out to debunk it. I fortunately had a strong mother in my corner, and a wonderful male mentor in my boss, Mayor Ronald O. Loveridge, the then-Mayor of Riverside, who gave me space to take the time and the encouragement to believe in myself. I resonate so much with how quickly these accomplished authors got right to the heart of this myth in Chapter 2, citing literary works such as "Nice Girls Don't Get the Corner Office," and "The Confidence Code." Add to that one of my favorites, "The Power of

Nice," the bestselling book by PR experts Linda Kaplan Thaler and Robin Koval who generously endorsed my own book on kindness. Collectively, these works helped normalize and encourage women, and men, to come forth in droves to let their nice flag fly to show how supporting others creates the virtuous cycle of support, reciprocity, and connecting.

Naturally, whenever I'm asked to give a talk to entrepreneurs, or others, on pretty much any topic, I start and end with relationship building, reciprocity and connecting (read: kindness) as key takeaways. Fast forward about 20 years and some twists and turns in my life, I've recently started to label myself the Occasional Entrepreneur. Because, looking back, I can see many times when I've embraced the need for something more inspirational, something different, something that was lacking in the traditional mantle of success I thought I had to pick up.

I'm often asked some version of, "what's your best advice for succeeding in today's competitive

world?"

My message now to all young women is simply to say 'Yes.'

"Yes" to anything and everything that truly tugs at your heart strings. Almost equally so, say "Yes" to those things that scare you the most. There is usually a reason that you're feeling so challenged by the very thing that you so want to manifest. Hint: because it matters. A lot.

Interested in volunteering on a campaign for a mayoral candidate you believe in even though you're busy meeting your high school class requirements? "Yes."

Want to be the social media manager for a small technology start up even if it requires you to take a year off of college? "Yes."

Go on that semester abroad when a diversity-based grant is going to pay your way, even though you're scared you might not measure up to the students who didn't need the grant to go? "Heck, Yes!"

Deathly afraid of speaking in public but know that your dream of starting an ethnic cafe in the

rundown neighborhood you grew up in won't happen if you don't learn to pitch to get investors?

So what do you say to the invitation to join the local Toastmasters International public speaking group? "Yes."

Ask the guest speaker who talked to your community group about Leadership Lessons to become your mentor, even though you are embarrassed to even ask a leader to help you?

"Yes."

"Yes" your way to success!

"Leading the Charge for Change" is not just about inspiring girls to become leaders, but also about providing actionable steps, a recipe that women can follow and add their special touches, to mentor and support the next generation. From networking advice to mentorship programs, these two accomplished professionals cover both the strategic and emotional aspects of helping young girls reach their full potential. Consistently helping build up young womens' confidence, accurately identifying, and then helping them battle their fears is crucial.

I remember being rocked by a quote, this one from Marianne Williamson's book, "A Return to Love," (but attributed to "The Course in Miracles"), which has been oft-quoted for its thought-provoking nature on facing our actual fears:

"Our deepest fear is not that we are inadequate. Our deepest fear is that we are powerful

beyond measure.It is our light, not our darkness that most frightens us. We ask ourselves, Who am I to be brilliant, gorgeous, talented, fabulous? Actually, who are you not to be? You are a child of God. Your playing small does not serve the world. There is nothing enlightened about shrinking so that other people won't feel insecure around you. We are all meant to shine, as children we do.

[sic]... And as we let our own light shine, we unconsciously give other people permission to do the same. As we are liberated from our own fear, our presence automatically liberates others."

Remember, the future belongs to those who are willing to step up and make a difference. I know that, as readers of this entertaining yet comprehensive book, you will be inspired to take charge, to become a leader, a change maker, and a role-model for young women around the world.

Together, we can inspire the next generation of female leaders and show them that they too can take charge, be the change, and make history.

So make that cup of coffee or tea, settle in and let this book envelop you in its unique storytelling and educating grasp. You don't catch a book like this very often.

Kristin Tillquist, LL.B

Innovator/Government Leader/Attorney/Author

"Capitalizing on Kindness: Why 21st Century Professionals Need to Be Nice"

INTRODUCTION

"She who dares to lead, ignites a spark that sets the world ablaze with possibilities."

– Unknown

It has been said that it takes a village to raise a child, and when it comes to raising future female leaders, the same concept applies. Tackling change, being a force for good, and striving to make a difference can be and oftentimes is a daunting task. Having a network of formal and informal mentors is a 'village' of like minded individuals that provides a sense of belonging which is key for providing women a foundation, encouragement, and support that is needed for their growth as leaders.

What shift might be made in village dynamics to ensure that a holistic network of both men and women's voices are in place and aware of the role they play in creating positive change in raising our future women leaders? What mindset shift needs to transpire?

"How strange that even a very minor event, action, or small shift can have such a tremendous effect. Like a butterfly's wing is capable of altering the path of a tornado, certainly everything, every event, the very tiny thing can affect

everything" Tuwalily.

In 2013, Sheryl Sandberg, the Facebook Chief Operating Officer created a cultural shift regarding women's role in the workplace and society with her best-selling book, *Lean In.* Sanberg's *pull yourself up to the table movement* inspired women to believe not only that they could achieve, but first women had to realize that they needed to be bold enough to claim a spot at the table, speak up, and take matters into their own hands. This movement was an awakening for women, re-writing the future of leadership; one that includes women, not as *token representatives*, but as valued partners and contributors.

Creating future female leaders requires more than simply *leaning in* and pulling a chair up to the table; it requires that women show up in a new way. It's about women encouraging and supporting other women to find their voice and lead with courage, but that's often easier said than done. How do we instill confidence and break down fear and stereotypical norms?

Designing a new path forward is about women leading the way, charting a course for others, and showing that it doesn't matter if it's never been done before. Crucial to inspiring and motivating the next generation of female leaders is the active involvement of other women and the sharing of their lived experiences. The cause for change happens by taking action and creating a new reality for future generations to come.

Change happens when we refuse to accept the status quo and the way things have always been. To change our communities and the world, women's understanding of their role in this change is paramount to leading the future. The ironic paradigm is that women have always been responsible for educating, influencing, and leading but often fail to recognize the significance of their role in shaping others and society.

We set out to understand the irony of how women don't necessarily see themselves as curators of the future. We hoped that asking these women to share their stories would reveal insights that could be used to help young women avoid some common pitfalls, self-imposed limits and provide them with a clear picture of possibility. It then became apparent that women are only part of the canvas and the inclusion of men's stories would be necessary to complete the painting. Without additional colors and brush strokes, we envisioned an incomplete work.

We wondered, if we were to take a poll of men and women, in any setting, and ask them if they had been positively influenced by a female in their lives, what role did natural characteristics of compassion, empathy, and nurturing play in their influence? What other characteristics do women possess that are necessary to facilitate leading people into action? How do these characteristics set the stage for impacting change?

"If you can't feed a hundred people, feed just one," Mother Teresa.

Any one of us may simply reflect on the positive influence of our own mother or a female teacher or public figure to understand the significance of women in our lives. We may think of the strength and wisdom of our grandmother and its impact. We can consider examples of the unwavering commitment of women like Mother Teresa, taking it upon herself to address human suffering. We cannot help but feel inspired by the graceful compassion and dedication that Princess Diana showed for people with HIV/Aids, disabled people, children and the homeless as she tirelessly provided love and support.

Our focus on women and their role as natural change-makers and leaders is especially timely as we continue, as a society, to give a voice to the voiceless, take a stand for justice, equality, peace, and sustainability. We are at a crossroads of a swinging pendulum of extremes and ideology of all or nothing. We have come so far, yet have so much farther to go.

Ceilings are being shattered, but are there supports in place to protect women from the shards of glass as it rains down?

The potential impact of women on lives and society becomes even more poignant when we look at their growing influence as business executives and corporate board members. Globally, women hold 35% of senior leadership positions, compared to 65% held by men. As of 2021, only 8.2% of Fortune 500 companies leaders were women, and for good reason, women bring unique qualities to the boardroom and decision-making. We wanted to understand what those were to help educate others, building momentum in women's leadership.

In the 1960s and 70s women that held elected positions within the U.S. Congress and House of Representatives were scarce. Although a steady increase of female representation exists, and despite women representing nearly half of the labor force, the ratio of men to women leaders is alarming. Worldwide, ninety percent of companies have at least one woman in a senior leadership role (Catalyst, 2022). Why the disparity? Why aren't women equally fulfilling these roles? This book will not only address these questions and provide insight, but will also provide solutions to help reverse any negative trajectory.

"Over the past five years, the number of women board members has increased by 18%" (Pay Governance, 2021). By 2019, 42% of all businesses in the United States were women owned. Of significant interest, "Women-owned businesses have higher failure rates, lower business value, and limited growth potential as compared to men-owned businesses (GEM, 2020). This begs several questions:

1) Why is this the case?

2) What is or is not happening for these women?

3) How can women be better supported in their career, business, academic, and personal aspirations?

4) How can we inspire and instill a sense of pride in young women so that they are prepared to thrive in their roles as leaders?

Women are leading the charge for change from a varying backgrounds, ages, and in a variety of ways. How can it be that women, who are leaders in the community, don't always see themselves as leaders? Everyday, *ordinary* women are accomplishing *extraordinary* things. This book is an exploration, celebration, and an illumination of the beauty that women bring to the canvas with colors, textures and caring attention to detail to create a better world.

Our hope is that these stories will inspire our next generation of women to be bold and brave and unafraid to be the change that they want to see in the world.

Ladies, on a daily basis we are leading the charge for change. We are standing up for our children, making sure our neighborhoods are safe, serving our communities as volunteers, elected officials and caregivers. Each of us have the abilities, skills and individual power that we can leverage to be better, grow, and learn. Our young people and society need to see us in leadership roles. We are high performing businesses executives, breaking ground as entreprenuers, managing our homes, and reimagining non-profit organizations. Ladies, we are now, we are the future, and we are inspiration!

It's time to better understand how change, dynamic, impactful, life-impacting change is curated, encouraged, developed, nurtured, inspired, birthed, and grown to thrive. It's time to realize that permission is not needed to step up and change the world around us. We don't have to wait for change, we are the change. The key is, the role that we, as women, have is to understand that our unity and support for one another is our driving force and the catalyst to lead the charge for change through inspiration.

For over two years we have conducted hundreds of formal and informal interviews with men and women from around the globe. We've engaged in deep conversations and solicited insights through social media and industry groups about women's role influencing and leading change. We've explored challenges that women have overcome and how they were encouraged to persevere. We asked for thoughts on solutions and what is needed for a better future.

What we didn't do was focus on CEO's of major corporations, multi-millionaires or celebrities. Instead, we asked "ordinary women" who are doing what they do, "extraordinary things," how they achieved, who helped them, and what they experienced along the way. We asked men for their thoughts. Who inspired them, how they see their role in supporting women, and what special qualities women bring to leadership, decision making and impacting change.

This book is a culmination of those conversations and experiences. We have summarized the stories, quotes, and tidbits of information into something meaningful, inspirational, and actionable, with hopes that one of you or anyone, at any age will be inspired to be an active member of your village and advance future women leaders.

Exploring the significance of female leadership in today's rapidly evolving world, we analyze the unique qualities and strengths that women bring to the table and highlight their role as powerful agents of change. By understanding the importance of empowering female leaders, all may be inspired to take on leadership roles and contribute positively to their communities.

What You Will Learn:

- How female leadership is essential for creating a more inclusive, equitable, and diverse society.

- How women can learn from trailblazing female leaders of the past to overcome challenges and break barriers.

- How developing an empowering mindset, effective communication, and negotiation skills are key to success in leadership.

- How building a supportive network, maintaining work-life balance, and practicing self-care are crucial for personal and professional growth.

- How adapting leadership styles and strategies to different situations can lead to better outcomes.

- How creating an inclusive and diverse work environment benefits all employees and fosters innovation.

- How encouraging diversity and inclusivity in academia fosters innovation and contributes to a broader range of perspectives and ideas.

- How nurturing the next generation of female leaders is crucial for continued progress towards gender equality.

CHAPTER 1

HISTORICAL CONTEXT OF WOMEN IN LEADERSHIP

"The legacy of a trailblazing woman is not only the barriers she breaks but the doors she opens for others to follow."

– Ruth Bader Ginsburg

Surveying the landscape of women's leadership, we are presented with an awe-inspiring panorama of audacious women who brazenly defied societal norms. Unyielding figures like Susan B. Anthony and Elizabeth Cady Stanton, who dared to dream of women's suffrage, or Malala Yousafzai, a voice for girls' education against daunting odds, have shown us that 'impossible' is a notion to be challenged and overcome. With their grit and spirit, they etched a path for future generations of female leaders to journey upon.

Our voyage commences in the footsteps of these formidable heroines, whose life stories of triumph and turmoil serve as guiding stars for future generations of women.

We aim to stir that latent spark in you, kindling the courage to venture beyond the horizon and be the harbinger of positive change.

We often extol the courageous acts of known heroines, such as Rosa Parks, who refused to yield her seat on a racially segregated bus in Montgomery, Alabama, in December of 1955. This single act of defiance ignited the Montgomery Bus Boycott, a 381-day protest that culminated in the Supreme Court declaring segregation on public buses unconstitutional. Parks' unyielding stand against racial injustice earmarked her as an enduring symbol of the Civil Rights Movement and a beacon of hope for women advocating change against tremendous odds. As we tread towards a future lit by the glow of female leadership, we must draw strength from inspiring figures like Parks, while also shining a light on less-known, yet equally momentous, champions of change.

Delving into the depths of female leadership, we are compelled to acknowledge the inestimable contributions of trailblazers like Rosalind Franklin. Born in London in 1920, Franklin stepped into a world largely dominated by men, armed only with her insatiable intellect and unquenchable curiosity. Rising through the ranks, she established herself as a leading chemist and X-ray crystallographer.

Her groundbreaking work in DNA structure, captured through X-ray crystallography, is an invaluable contribution to science. While her pioneering efforts remained largely unrecognized during her lifetime, her indomitable spirit fuels the aspirations of young women globally, encouraging them to reach for the stars, despite the shadows of prejudice and discrimination.

Franklin's story and others like hers urge us not only to honor their remarkable achievements but also to nurture the rising wave of future female leaders. They serve as pillars of hard work, determination, and relentless pursuit of dreams, inspiring us to be architects of change and positively impact our world.

Rosalind died tragically young, at the age of 37, from ovarian cancer. However, her legacy lives on, inspiring generations of young women to pursue their passion for science and engineering. Her determination, intelligence, and unwavering commitment to her work continue to be a beacon of hope for women around the world who aspire to be difference makers.

Just as numbers enchanted a young Katherine Johnson in the 1930s, the narratives of these exceptional women are designed to captivate you. Despite the shackles of racism and societal discrimination, Johnson, armed with a fervor for mathematics, changed the trajectory of space travel. As an African-American woman working in a segregated unit of NACA, the precursor to NASA, she calculated the launch and landing trajectories for the first manned space flights by hand for white male counterparts. Her calculations were the success behind the historic mission, Apollo 11, that put the first human on the moon. Her indelible contributions to space science led to her numerous accolades, including the Presidential Medal of Freedom in 2015.

Katherine's impact extended far beyond her work on the space program. As a trailblazing African-American woman in a male-dominated field, she inspired generations of women and minorities to pursue careers in science, technology, engineering, and math. With the release of her story in the award-winning 2016 movie, Hidden Figures, her commitment and passion for science has inspired a new generation of women and minorities in STEM and this movement is expanding around the world. Katherine reminded us all that when talent is given the opportunity to shine, it can change the world.

Today, Katherine's legacy lives on through the countless young women and girls who are inspired by her story, and who are empowered to use their own talents and passions to make a positive difference in the world. She was a true leader in every sense of the word, and she blazed a trail for us all to follow.

As we weave through the fabric of women's leadership, we are introduced to Radia Perlman, another linchpin in the panorama of female pioneers. Perlman's inventions, particularly the Spanning Tree Algorithm, laid the groundwork for the modern internet. Her tireless innovation and unyielding spirit have not only transformed our digital lives but also kindled a beacon of inspiration for girls across the globe to venture into STEM fields.

Johnson and Perlman's stories resonate with the power of women leaders who defied the odds, further reiterating our belief that women's leadership is crucial in crafting our future. We must actively cultivate an environment that nurtures the budding potential of young women and molds them into the leaders of tomorrow.

The tale of physicist Chien-Shiung Wu, considered one of the greatest scientists of the twentieth century, is another embodiment of this spirit. Despite facing discrimination throughout her career, Wu's revolutionary experiments altered the course of physics.

In 1956, Wu conducted an experiment that would change the course of physics forever. The Wu experiment disproved the hypothetical law of conservation of parity, a fundamental principle that had been widely accepted for decades. Wu's groundbreaking work paved the way for new discoveries and challenged long-held beliefs about the nature of our universe.

Despite her immense contributions to science, Wu faced significant discrimination throughout her career. In 1957, she was overlooked for the Nobel Prize in Physics, which was instead awarded to her male colleagues. This injustice sparked outrage and led the way for a renewed focus on gender equality in science.

Wu's legacy lives on today, inspiring countless young women around the world to pursue their dreams and push past barriers. As women leaders, it is our responsibility to nurture the next generation and ensure that they have the support and resources they need to succeed. By raising up young women and empowering them to make a positive impact on the world, we can continue the work of trailblazers like Chien-Shiung Wu and create a brighter future for all.

Dame Stephanie Shirley, another unsung heroine, carved a path for women in the technology industry by founding a successful software company, Freelance Programmers in the 1960s. Through her company, she afforded opportunities to many women in a male-dominated industry, showcasing the immense potential women possess to disrupt the status quo and forge a path of their own. Over the years, her company grew to employ over 8,500 people, many of them women who had been given opportunities they never thought possible. Hiring primarily women, she broke barriers and paved the way for a new generation of female technologists to enter the field.

Dame Stephanie's passion for social issues didn't stop at the door of her business, either. She has long been a champion for autism research and treatment, and founded the Shirley Foundation to support this cause. Over the years, the Foundation has made significant contributions to research, education, and treatment for autism, helping to make a real difference in the lives of countless families.

Through her leadership, innovation, and commitment to social change, Dame Stephanie Shirley has been an inspiration to women across the globe. Her legacy reminds us of the power of a single person to make a difference, and the importance of empowering the next generation of leaders to continue that work.

Their unwavering determination and resilience act as torches in the uncharted territory of women's leadership. They illuminate the path for future generations, encouraging them to persevere, fight for equality, and be a force of positive change in the world.

In this vast galaxy of women's leadership, every star – every woman – has left an indelible mark on society, a testament to the potential that exists within each of us. Let us follow the constellations they have formed in the infinite cosmos of opportunities, and be the comet that initiates the change we wish to see in the world.

The legacy of women's leadership is a brilliant tapestry woven with threads of resilience, determination, and promise. This legacy is the guiding light for future generations, inspiring women to fight against all odds, challenge norms, and create a better world for all. As leaders of today, our task is to ensure this light is never extinguished but handed down from generation to generation, nurturing the pathfinders of tomorrow.

Let the stories of these women be the clarion call to action. A world of opportunities awaits those who dare to dream and are brave enough to follow their convictions. Let us carry forth the legacy of these audacious women, refusing to accept defeat and taking the lead in initiating change. Our journey into the annals of women's leadership is a testament to their resilience, determination, and enormous potential. Let their stories inspire you to break barriers, strive for equality, and be a beacon of change for all.

Taking Action

Strategies for Learning from the Past

Building upon the legacies of the incredible women

who have paved the way for us, we must acknowledge that carrying their torch into the future involves more than just acknowledging their efforts - it requires us to take conscious, tangible steps.

Action, however, can often feel overwhelming - where does one even begin? It starts with learning from the past and translating these lessons into strategies that can help shape the leaders of tomorrow. The following sections will guide you through a set of concrete actions that can be applied to cultivate leadership skills, inspired by the women leaders we've highlighted earlier in this chapter.

Encourage self-confidence and self-awareness

Developing self-confidence and self-awareness in young women is crucial to prepare them for leadership roles. When mentors instill a strong sense of self-belief, young women become more resilient, able to express themselves effectively, and better equipped to handle challenging situations. Self-awareness helps them understand their strengths, weaknesses, and areas for growth, enabling them to make informed decisions and lead authentically.

Take inspiration from Rosa Parks - stand up for what you believe in and don't underestimate the power of your voice. Self-confidence isn't about being the loudest in the room, but having the courage to express your thoughts and views, even when they go against the grain.

On the other hand, self-awareness is about knowing your strengths and weaknesses, just as Rosalind Franklin did. She recognized her brilliance in the sciences and pursued it passionately, regardless of the lack of recognition. Regularly take time to reflect on your strengths, weaknesses, values, and passions. Seek feedback from mentors, peers, and colleagues to gain additional perspectives.

Provide opportunities for skill development

Mentors should expose young women to a variety of skill-building opportunities to help them develop their leadership abilities. This includes opportunities for public speaking, negotiation, teamwork, critical thinking, and problem-solving. By acquiring a diverse skill set, young women are empowered to take on leadership roles with confidence and competence.

As Radia Perlman did, seize every opportunity to enhance your skills. Whether it's technical knowledge or soft skills like negotiation and public speaking, continuous learning is an essential component of leadership. Make use of online courses, workshops, and mentoring programs to improve existing skills and learn new ones.

Foster an inclusive and supportive environment

Mentors must create an inclusive and supportive environment where young women feel comfortable expressing their thoughts and opinions. This cultivates a sense of belonging and encourages active participation in decision-making processes. By promoting diversity and inclusivity, mentors demonstrate that all voices are important and valuable, empowering young women to share their unique perspectives as leaders.

Leaders like Dame Stephanie Shirley created environments where women could flourish, even in fields dominated by men. We should strive to do the same. Encourage open and inclusive conversations, promote diversity, and ensure everyone feels valued. Supportive environments foster creativity, collaboration, and respect - qualities that are central to effective leadership.

Highlight positive role models

Showcasing positive female role models in leadership positions is vital for inspiring the next generation of young women leaders. By seeing other women succeed, young women can visualize their own potential and develop a sense of self-efficacy. Mentors should also emphasize the importance of having both male and female role models, highlighting the benefits of diverse perspectives in leadership.

Having women leaders to look up to can be incredibly inspiring. Just as Katherine Johnson's story continues to inspire young women in STEM fields, you can inspire others by being a role model yourself or bringing attention to women leaders in your communities and industries. These role models provide a vision of what is achievable, challenging societal norms, and inspiring future generations.

Encourage collaboration and networking

Building strong relationships and networks is essential for success in any field. Mentors should encourage young women to collaborate with peers, engage with professionals in their areas of interest, and join relevant organizations or clubs. This helps young women develop strong interpersonal skills and expand their professional networks, paving the way for future leadership opportunities.

Develop a network that supports your leadership journey. Collaboration with like-minded individuals and organizations can open doors to new opportunities and ideas. It also helps in building communication and interpersonal skills, which are crucial for leadership roles.

Address and challenge gender stereotypes

Mentors play a key role in addressing and challenging

gender stereotypes that can hinder young women's leadership potential. By discussing these stereotypes and encouraging young women to defy societal expectations, mentors help dismantle barriers that prevent women from taking on leadership roles. Open and honest conversations about gender equality and biases are essential in fostering a more equitable future for all.

Much like Chien-Shiung Wu, be aware of and challenge the gender stereotypes that might limit you or other women. These stereotypes often deter women from pursuing leadership roles. Addressing and challenging these stereotypes begins with conversation and education.

Provide feedback and guidance

Regular feedback and guidance from mentors is essential for the growth and development of young women as leaders. Constructive feedback helps them recognize their strengths and identify areas for improvement, while guidance offers direction and support in overcoming obstacles. Mentors should emphasize that learning and growth are lifelong processes, empowering young women to continuously improve and adapt as they pursue leadership roles.

Leaders grow through constant feedback and improvement. Seek out feedback on your performance, much like Katherine Johnson did during her time at

NASA. And as a leader, provide the same for those in your charge. Constructive feedback can inspire growth, improvement, and encourage continuous learning as it provides a sense of direction.

Engage with inspiring female-led projects on social media

The digital era provides an array of platforms that allow us to engage with the work of contemporary female leaders, just as the trailblazers of the past connected with each other. Following their lead, we can learn from their experiences and actively support their initiatives.

Platforms such as LinkedIn, Facebook, and Instagram serve as virtual meeting spaces where we can witness the continuation of the work started by our trailblazers. Here, we can find a myriad of female-led initiatives that are reshaping industries, challenging the status quo, and breaking new ground, much like Rosa Parks, Radia Perlman, Dame Stephanie Shirley, Katherine Johnson, and Chien-Shiung Wu did in their respective fields.

By actively engaging with these initiatives, we're not only gaining insight into the modern landscape of women in leadership but also becoming a part of a supportive network.

This network is similar to the ones that our trailblazers created and relied on for information, inspiration, and support.

These digital platforms also enable us to support these modern trailblazers in their journeys. Just as our historical trailblazers championed each other's causes, we can use social media to amplify the messages of today's female leaders, join their causes, and contribute to their campaigns.

Moreover, we can follow in the footsteps of our trailblazers by using these platforms to challenge gender stereotypes, much like Chien-Shiung Wu did in her time. Today's platforms provide an opportunity to share stories, challenge biases, and bring visibility to the work of women leaders around the globe.

Finally, just as Katherine Johnson sought feedback to improve her work, we can utilize these platforms for constructive dialogue, sharing ideas, and receiving feedback.

In essence, engaging with female-led initiatives on these platforms is an extension of the interconnectedness and mutual support that our trailblazing women leaders demonstrated. It serves as a modern way to carry their torch, lighting the way for future women leaders.

Collaborate with local organizations promoting gender parity

Mentors can encourage young women to join forces with local organizations working towards gender parity in education and employment sectors. This not only helps raise awareness about existing inequalities but also provides opportunities for young women to develop essential skills, gain practical experience, and understand the importance of collective action in driving change. Collaboration with these organizations also expands their network and connects them with like-minded individuals who share a passion for gender equality.

Working with organizations that advocate for women's leadership can provide invaluable experiences. These collaborations can give you practical tools, resources, and platforms to further your leadership journey.

Empower young women to dream big and believe in their potential

Mentors should inspire young women to set ambitious goals and believe in their ability to achieve them. By fostering a "can-do" attitude and emphasizing the importance of persistence, mentors help young women build the resilience and determination necessary to overcome obstacles and reach their full potential.

Encouraging young women to dream big not only increases their self-confidence but also motivates them to push boundaries and strive for excellence, essential qualities in any leader.

Finally, take a page from the book of every woman leader who has left her mark on history - dream big and persevere. Leaders are often faced with enormous challenges, but their vision and determination propel them forward. Let the stories of these women leaders remind you of what you can achieve and inspire you to keep moving forward, no matter the hurdles you face.

Implementing these actions requires commitment and perseverance, but remember, every step you take is a step towards a future where women's leadership is celebrated and encouraged. This roadmap is not an exhaustive list; it is a starting point. It's up to each of us to take action in our unique way, using the tools and platforms available to us. Let's honor the legacy of the women who paved the way by continuing their work and fostering a new generation of women leaders.

Key Takeaways

- Women trailblazers have contributed significantly to various fields, often overcoming significant challenges and breaking stereotypes.

- The accomplishments of these trailblazing women demonstrate the potential and importance of female representation in all areas of society.

- Recognizing the achievements of lesser-known female trailblazers helps to raise awareness and inspire future generations of women to pursue their ambitions.

- It is crucial to address the historical erasure and underappreciation of women's contributions in order to create a more equitable and inclusive understanding of our past.

- The stories of these trail blazers highlight the need for continued efforts in dismantling barriers and providing support for women in all fields, ensuring that their work is valued and recognized.

CHAPTER 2

EMPOWERING MINDSETS FOR FEMALE LEADERS

"Women who lead the charge for change are the architects of a brighter, more inclusive future for all."

– Michelle Obama

In the journey of leadership, women don't just set the path for themselves; they forge it for countless others who aspire to rise. Your endeavors and successes aren't just personal victories – they are the beacon lights that guide the aspirations of subsequent generations of female leaders. However, traversing the path of leadership is no cakewalk. Historically, the corridors of power have been littered with barriers and deterrents – many a result of a cultural paradigm that systematically marginalized women, fostering a toxic competitive environment.

Globally, women account for just 35% of senior leadership roles. Delving into the experiences of these trailblazing women provides a lens into the adversities they've faced. When posed with the question of which barriers need to be toppled to reshape the landscape of female leadership, a plethora of enlightening insights surfaced, further deepened by extensive interviews.

"The language used to describe strong women" is a barrier that needs to be overcome. Stacy Thompson, Supervisor of Administrative Services, Bay Area of California.

"The barrier of the belief that women can't have it all; good health, family, ambition, passion; all can coexist harmoniously!" Priya Mishra, Manager, Accenture Technologies.

To bridge these voices, Dr. Elizabeth Church, Director of Science Programs, offers a perspective from the world of academia and scientific leadership. She states, "Competition might not fairly reward the strengths of all genders, if there are no objective measures on which to evaluate the end product and all genders are not included as evaluators. Furthermore, a type of competition exists which benefits no one, one that promotes redundant efforts in the absence of transparency. In such a scenario, I immediately cease to contribute when I learn that another has been assigned the same task. This redundancy is demoralizing."

This chapter takes a deep dive into the many trials and tribulations women leaders frequently encounter. From battling ingrained gender biases and stereotypes that often make women second-guess their capabilities to confronting overt and covert hurdles, leadership can be a daunting journey. But every cloud has a silver lining. We will not only discuss the problems but also provide actionable solutions. Strategies that help the emerging generation of female leaders to rise above these challenges, fortified with self-belief.

We will spotlight quintessential leadership attributes: self-confidence, ambition, resilience, and more. Accompanied by what specific actions can be taken and key insights, this chapter aims to nurture and amplify these traits in aspiring leaders of any age. By its conclusion, you'll be armed not only with insights into the often unassuming, yet powerful characteristics of female leadership but also with an arsenal of strategies to surmount them.

Now, let's embark on this transformative journey, equipping ourselves and the subsequent wave of female leaders for a brighter future!

Who Am I to Change the World?

Be strong; you never know who you are inspiring.

It was a hope-filled day as Stacy Shewey rang the bell in the cancer center. The end of radiation and the end of a battle. A beautiful sunny summer day in Florida, this should have been a time of elation, relief, and celebration. Instead, this was a bittersweet hurdle in an often-cruel world. Just ten weeks prior Stacy, mother of three, had been delivered a one-two punch. On Thursday she had cancer surgery, and on Sunday lost her beloved son Alex in a tragic accident. Nothing could have prepared her for either, the latter, even more devastating than the first.

The magnitude of the events within just a few days of each other would serve as a knock-out blow, to just throw in the towel, for just about anyone. It would have been easy to just give up, but Stacy credits her faith in God, friends, family, and complete strangers for helping her "carry the burden of sickness and grief."

"I have a choice right now to face the light and not walk in the shadows. If I don't put my faith into action, I will not be able to get out of bed, stay of sound mind, and continue my work," Stacy professed as she left the hospital that day.

Stacy knew from a young age that she was "meant to do something great," yet like most of us, experienced the limiting thought, "But who am I?"

Stacey admits to her weakness, like so many other women.

- Who am I?
- I'm just average.

- Who am I to do something great?
- Who am I to bring about change?
- Who am I to think that I can change the world?
- What do I know?
- I'm not smart enough.
- I'm too old.

Searching for a fit and believing that her past executive experience owning and operating boutique hotels and properties, as well as years as a top performer in corporate sales would provide relevant work experience and skills to serve in an executive role in nearly any industry, Stacy found herself drawn to elderly care. Accepting a position as Director of an assisted living facility in Florida, Stacy fell in love with the residents, their stories, and the role she served in providing care. Soon she gained a keen awareness of flaws in the system and society's disregard for our aging population. People seemed to be stored away like unused household items, placed out of sight, and often out of mind. She points to an aging crisis wherein seniors are considered inherently less valuable as they age.

"There was a time when our Asian and Indian cultures did a great job, caring for their elders, but even that is changing," explains Shewey. "We need to teach our younger generations the circle of life. Our parents once cared for us and then as the circle completes, we care for our aging parents."

Three years prior to Alex's death, at age 51, Stacy had stepped away from her director role and took a leap of faith, founding Hands4Life, a non-profit focused on globally changing how assisted living for the elderly is addressed. With 62% of people over the age of 60 living in developing countries, that number is projected to increase to 80%. Hands4Life was born with a vision to solve the senior care crisis holistically and systemically at its core. Created by a woman, with no background in running a non-profit, let alone a global organization, Stacy just knew that something had to be done and her "Who am I to do this," became, "Who am I not to?"

"I've never been afraid to take risks, to embrace a mission and vision and to step out in faith. Risks lead to us leading a fulfilled life. I may not be successful at all ventures, but it will be an adventure." Even so, Stacy humbly admits, "I'm not doing anything great. I'm just a connector. People are coming to me saying, "How can I help?"

Stacy thinks of herself as an *ordinary woman*. She is anything but. Her organization is reinventing assisted living by looking at the entire picture, not just honing in on elderly care. Hands4Life is dedicated to developing model communities around the world, with a particular focus on those that have been cast out of sight by society, orphans young and old.

Developed nations are taking notice as Hands4Life implements a single sustainable community model in each country around the world. "Foreign organizations can often harm the nationals by imposing their cultural values, norms, and corporate rules. Our model provides one project per country to serve as a training ground to empower the next generation. It is up to the individual governments to then replicate the model throughout their countries and put systems in place to promote sustainable communities that address hunger, housing, and care for all."

Stacy, surrounded by global thought leaders on elderly care and senior living, has designed communities wherein the young and old hold reverence for their role in the community. The young learn crafts from their elders. The elders impart wisdom and feel valued, respected, and revered. Not only is the problem of orphan children that are cast out onto the streets at eighteen without job skills or money, falling prey to human traffickers, crime, and prostitution being addressed, but the model provides for intergenerational cooperation and collaboration to fulfill the circle of life. The model connects basic needs, clean water, food, and shelter with a sense of community, belonging, and dignity. The elders are honored for the past wherein the youth are empowered for the future.

Stacy knew she was supposed to do something great. She didn't know what it was or how. She's lived through sexism and female stereotype dispersion in male dominated workforces. She's been asked to make appointments and serve as a pseudo-secretary, even being asked to re-write the Rolodex of a male peer, whom she was supposed to be equal.

"We've come a long way, but we have a long way to go," says Stacy, "to achieve what we want to achieve. I'm usually the one leading the business, yet in certain situations I find myself having my husband have conversations with certain men that I know don't see me as someone of authority. It's frustrating that they see me as that *little lady*," not as the head of a global non-profit.

Stacy credits her boldness to take the leap of faith to a male business leader who dared her to dream, understand the why of her dream and helped connect her to resources to make her dream a reality. She surrounds herself with people who can provide support, whether an advocate and cheerleader or a sounding board and provider of feedback.

Stacy's wish for our future generations of females is that they would not need to know terms like girl power and glass ceilings, that they would find that a book discussing such things would be the craziest thing ever. That they would say, "What was going on with these people? They had to write a book about this?" She feels it's sad that we must have these conversations, yet "we need to start at the beginning and not the end. We need to change the dialogue and create new messaging between men and women. Just like we need to change the thinking on both ends of the spectrum between young and old. Both have value. Intergenerational is powerful." The village is powerful.

Stacy's story is important as it clearly illustrates how women, within their everyday life functions, see themselves as ordinary. She sees herself as "just normal." In her role as a mother, she is modeling leadership and serving as a role model beyond her family and community but on a global scale. She is changing the world and impacting the quality of life for those in developing countries who had no hope. Although Alex, "Shewey", as his friends referred to him, did not get to see the legacy his mother is leaving on this world come to fruition, I'm sure he's smiling down from heaven saying, "You got this mom. You go girl!"

It's a reality, leadership is hard. Regardless of whether you fall into the camp that leaders are born rather than leaders are made. A sad reality is that as women we have had to fight harder for everything we have accomplished. However, what's beautiful is that we quite often don't know how, but we know we will. It's an intuitive optimism in the greater good that helps us look differently at how we see the bigger picture and how we've overcome stereotypes and gender barriers. It's quite frankly, an aspect that over and over again our conversations with men and women have revealed and an indication into why more and more women are choosing to lead the charge for change. So why is this so important? What does it mean to our future generations? Why should we care?

We are at a prime juncture in history where the convergence of social, environmental, technological, spiritual and political pressures are driving extreme positioning amongst groups of people. Personal beliefs, ideologies and past mistakes contribute to the writing on the wall are all fueling an insistent desire in humanity to resolve injustices and imbalance. The time could never be more right than now to illuminate a path for young women, helping provide them a smoother road than that of past generations.

We've fought so very hard for fundamental rights such as equality, experiencing set-backs, frustrations, and disappointments along the way, yet we continue trudging forward with a renewed perspective, intentionality, and persistence. We focus on how the world should look for our sons and daughters, the masterpiece is one free of prejudice, with limitless possibilities and respect for one another. What we choose to eliminate from the canvas are the shackles of stereotypical roles and gender-based barriers.

Vicki Lynch, an advocate and board member for the disabled, shared of a time early in her retail management career wherein she was adversely impacted by a stereotype of male leadership. She explains, "If I would come on the phone or to the counter following a request for a manager, the customer would look confused and would insist that they wanted to see the real manager, the male manager. I was the only manager on duty and it was difficult because I knew that I was just as qualified as the men, and often, I was more qualified."

Seven months after giving birth to her son, Emotus founder and CEO, Angela Giacoumis, was faced with a dilemma that has taxed women for decades. Angela hoped to scale back her hours upon returning to work, enabling her to strike a balance between spending time with her son, other family obligations and earning a living.

"Going back to work full-time was the only option the organization provided so I decided to write my own way. I just did it. I quit my job. It was 1991 and we were in a recession. People thought I was crazy but I've never looked back." Angela founded Careerlink People Solutions, later selling the $10M company and then founding Emotus where she focuses on helping organizational leaders refocus on how they can help their people thrive.

Like so many women, Angela was left with no choice but to choose between her employment and motherhood. What's asinine is that it's not like women have not just started giving birth, yet businesses, governments, and society are barely scratching the surface in identifying sustainable solutions that don't leave women with all or nothing. Equity pay laws to address employment gaps, hybrid work options, job sharing, and on-site daycare are only partial solutions in the eradication of barriers for mothers.

Ladies, we are the catalyst for change. You never know who is watching or who will be inspired by your actions to take action. The question is, who are you NOT to change the world? It's time to unapologetically seize the moment and lead the charge for change.

As we examine the lives of these women and their triumphs, we must peel back the layers and ask ourselves, 'What lies at the heart of these achievements?' There is a common thread of resolve, a fiery ambition fueled by courage.

Stacy Shewey's story is one such story, laced with strength and determination. She faced life's cruelest blows with grace and a spirit that refused to bow. Her journey paints the picture of a woman of faith, one who trusts in her vision and isn't afraid of the risks associated with it. But let's dig deeper.

"Nice Girl's Don't Get the Corner Office ", Lois P. Frankel's insight into the unconscious mistakes women make reveals that women like Stacy often feel average, questioning their right to change the world. The prevalent thought, "Who am I to do something great?", "Who am I to bring about change?", frequently robs women of their true potential. However, Stacy turned this around, rephrasing the question to, "Who am I not to?"

In our society, traditional gender roles and societal expectations often subconsciously guide women's actions. The admonishments of childhood - 'Be a nice girl,' 'Don't make a scene,' 'Don't be so ambitious,' - seep into our adult psyches. Frankel asks us to reexamine these conditioned reflexes, the 'nice girl' behaviors that can sabotage our careers. She advises us to not just question these traditional expectations but also challenge and reshape them.

Drawing from Katty Kay and Claire Shipman's "The Confidence Code," we learn that self-assurance is a critical ingredient in the recipe for success. They assert that women, more often than men, struggle with self-doubt, which can dampen their confidence. However, confidence is not simply handed over; it's built through action, risk-taking, and facing failure. Women like Stacy prove that one can foster confidence through persistence and resilience.

In this light, Stacy's faith in her vision and audacity to leap is nothing short of revolutionary. The development of Hands4Life is a testament to her courage to step outside her comfort zone, thus acting as an effective confidence-building exercise.

Further, the construction of Hands4Life communities and the nurturing of the young and old under one roof mirrors a dynamic shift. It dismantles the ingrained, traditional norms of society, where the old are forgotten, and the young are left to fend for themselves. Here, Stacy rebukes societal norms and, in their place, promotes intergenerational cooperation and respect, fostering a powerful, self-sustaining community.

Yet, despite these achievements, women like Vicki and Stacy have encountered gender bias, and even in her role as a global leader, Stacy was diminished to "the little lady." Like many women, both Vicki and Stacy have been undermined, not seen as an authoritative figure. Frankel's call to reject the 'nice girl' stereotype and Kay Shipman's emphasis on building confidence, resonate deeply here. They guide us on how to navigate such challenges, underscoring the need to assert ourselves firmly and confidently.

As we weave these threads together, our aim is to illuminate a path forward for women, showing them that they can defy stereotypes, build confidence, and lead in their unique ways. Women are not just 'nice girls'; they are architects of change, resilient warriors, and inspirational leaders. As we inspire the next generation, let's uphold this message, moving forward with determination and grace, just like Vicki and Stacy.

We are at a critical junction in history. It is a time to not only celebrate the achievements of women but also to recognize the systemic obstacles they have overcome. The dialogue has begun, and the canvas is slowly changing its hue. The real question is not, 'Who am I to change the world?' but 'Who am I not to?' Remember, every ripple counts, every whisper of change matters. Let's hold onto our vision and charge towards it with unflinching resolve. After all, the world needs more Vickis and Stacys. And it needs you, dear reader, to find your voice and make your mark.

Indeed, leadership is not an innate trait but a skill to

be honed and nurtured over time. The traits of successful leaders aren't gendered, yet often women face unique challenges that necessitate a distinct approach. Women don't need to lead as men do; they should embrace their leadership style that combines compassion, strength, and intelligence.

Through my narrative lens, I see the stories of women like Vicki and Stacy not as an exception, but as a testament to the strength and resilience that women possess. The exploration of the principles highlighted in the "The Confidence Code" and "Nice Girls Don't Get the Corner Office" sets the stage for further examination.

Leadership begins with confidence. As Katty Kay and Claire Shipman postulate, confidence is a cornerstone for success and an aspect where women often undervalue themselves. Yet, confidence isn't something that magically appears—it's built on the foundation of self-belief, risk-taking, and resilience.

Thus, to inspire the next generation of female leaders, we must foster an environment that encourages risk-taking and makes it safe to fail. Leaders like these become role models, showing that it's okay to take leaps of faith, to risk failure in pursuit of their dreams. As we cultivate confidence in our girls from an early age, we instill in them the courage to chase their aspirations.

A strategic way to foster this confidence is through mentorship and representation. Young women need to see leaders who look like them, who have walked the path they aspire to tread. If our young women see diverse representation in leadership roles, it gives them the affirmation that they too can be leaders in their chosen fields.

Let's use these real life examples and insights as a strategic framework for women's leadership. The unconscious mistakes women make, often due to societal conditioning, can be detrimental to their growth. Recognizing these patterns is the first step toward change.

As we gain a greater understanding of how the 'nice girl' stereotype can hinder women from asserting their authority, we can gain confidence in our role to inspire future generations. Many women feel compelled to be liked and approved of, often at the expense of their leadership potential. Breaking away from this need for approval and allowing oneself to take command, make unpopular decisions when necessary, and voice one's opinion is crucial. We need to teach our young women that being assertive is not being aggressive—it's about expressing oneself clearly and respectfully, demanding the respect they deserve.

Equally important is fostering a mindset that values

growth and continuous learning. No leader, regardless of their gender, knows everything. But what sets great leaders apart is their willingness to learn, adapt, and grow. By encouraging a growth mindset in our young women, we are preparing them to be future leaders who are adaptable, innovative, and resilient.

Lastly, we should underscore the importance of intersectionality in leadership. The challenges a woman faces are not just influenced by her gender but also by other aspects like race, ethnicity, social background, and more. By recognizing this, we are better equipped to nurture a more inclusive form of leadership, which is essential in our increasingly diverse world.

Leadership isn't just about leading—it's about inspiring, motivating, and influencing others. As we look to inspire the next generation of female leaders, we must give them the tools to be confident, resilient, and authentic leaders. The world doesn't just need more leaders; it needs more women leaders who lead with compassion, integrity, and courage. Let us endeavor to create an environment where this becomes a reality.

Taking Action

Strategies for Empowering the Mindset of Young Women

From Stacy's determination to Vicki's resilience, the experiences of both women lay a strong foundation for aspiring female leaders. They've demonstrated that the path to leadership is not linear, but rather a winding journey punctuated with triumphs, lessons, and unwavering persistence. Now, let's translate their combined experiences into a dynamic set of strategic actions aimed at empowering the mindset of young women.

Networking and Support Groups

Stacy and Vicki both knew the power of community in their leadership journeys. Embrace the same by engaging with women's professional organizations such as Lean In Circles, Ellevate Network, and the International Women's Leadership Association. Expand your professional circles through LinkedIn and local Meetup groups centered around women in leadership and industries that pique your interest.

Coaching and Mentoring

Both Stacy and Vicki benefited from mentorship that honed their leadership skills. Harness the wisdom of a career coach or mentor experienced in navigating women through the leadership labyrinth. Participate in programs designed specifically for women, like the Million Women Mentors initiative.

Building Mindfulness and Personal Development Practices

Stacy's focus and Vicki's self-awareness underscored the importance of mindfulness and personal development. Incorporate meditation, journaling, or visualization exercises into your daily routine to cultivate a mindset of self-awareness, confidence, and resilience. Adopt the practice of setting SMART goals, reviewing your progress regularly to ensure personal and professional growth.

What we can learn from Stacy and Vicki's narratives

- An empowering mindset is essential for overcoming barriers and succeeding in leadership roles.
- Qualities like self-confidence, ambition, and resilience are not inherent but can be nurtured and developed.
- Networks, mentorship programs, and professional development opportunities are invaluable resources for growth and career progression.

- Mindfulness and personal development practices contribute to better decision-making and an empowering mindset.

- An integrated action plan encompassing learning, networking, mentorship, and personal development can boost a woman's leadership journey and career success.

- The narratives of Stacy and Vicki, paired with these strategic actions, illuminate the path for the next generation of female leaders, equipping them to not only navigate but also redefine the contours of the leadership landscape.

What You Can Do

Networking and Support Groups

Women's professional organizations, such as Lean In Circles, Ellevate Network, and the International Women's Leadership Association.

LinkedIn groups and local Meetup groups focused on women in leadership or specific industries.

Coaching and Mentoring

Seeking guidance from a career coach or mentor experienced in helping women overcome barriers in leadership roles.

"Be like a zero. It might look insignificant as an absolute but when it joins hands with the rest, the impact is so powerful. Infinity has no limits," Priya Mishra.

Participating in mentorship programs specifically designed for women, such as the Million Women Mentors initiative.

Building Mindfulness and Personal Development Practices

Incorporating meditation, journaling, or visualization exercises into daily routines to help build self-awareness, confidence, and resilience.

Setting SMART goals (Specific, Measurable, Achievable, Relevant, and Time-bound) and regularly reviewing progress to stay focused on personal and professional growth.

Key Takeaways

- Developing an empowering mindset is crucial for women to overcome barriers and succeed in leadership roles.
- Building self-confidence, embracing ambition, and fostering resilience are essential qualities for female leaders and can be cultivated through various resources, tools, and practices.

- Engaging with supportive networks, mentorship programs, and professional development opportunities can help women grow and thrive in their careers.
- Mindfulness and personal development practices can contribute to a strong foundation for an empowering mindset and better decision-making.
- An action plan that incorporates learning, networking, mentorship, and personal development can greatly enhance a woman's leadership journey and overall career success.

CHAPTER 3

POWERFUL COMMUNICATION: FINDING YOUR VOICE

"The strength of a woman is not measured by her achievements but by her resilience in the face of adversity."

– Oprah Winfrey

If this resilience is the heart of a woman, communication and negotiation are her vocal chords, the conduit through which her thoughts and ideas resonate in the world. Often, as women, we don't realize the power of our voice and the positive impact it has on those around us. In this section, we take you on a journey of empowering your voice, not just to be heard, but to effect transformative change.

Bud Fish, Jr., Retired Architect, confidently explains that the women who had the most significant impact on his life were, his mother, then his wife, followed closely by his daughter. "All three always would always tell it like it is and all stood by me when others fell away." Now that is empowerment in action.

In the high-stakes world of leadership, mastering the

art of active listening, empathy, and assertiveness is imperative. Drawing from real-life experiences and practical advice, we will show you how to navigate power dynamics and challenging conversations, emboldening you to become a confident and persuasive communicator.

Authors Patterson, Grenny, McMillan, and Switzler, in their book Crucial Conversations: Tools for Talking When Stakes are High, emphasize the importance of creating a safe space in emotionally charged conversations. In an era where digital communication is rampant, young women must master the art of respectful, open communication. Techniques such as exploring others' beliefs and experiences to understand their viewpoints can pave the way for healthy, balanced discourse and counteract the marginalization of women's voices.

Gabriela Torres, a seasoned finance executive based in New York, offers invaluable wisdom on the art of dialogue and the subtleties of navigating disagreements in professional settings. She advises, "While you may not find common ground in every conversation, it's crucial to engage respectfully. Articulating your counterpoint with poise can go a long way, but what's often transformative is inviting the other person to elaborate on their perspective. This invitation is an act of respect that can pivot the entire tone of the discussion, opening pathways to deeper, more meaningful exchanges."

As women, our emotional strength is our unique asset, our 'Super Power'. Harnessing our emotional intelligence enables us to manage conflicts and disagreements constructively. It equips us to address high-stakes situations with resilience and assertiveness, characteristics crucial for successful leadership.

Adriana Malone, an adept project manager at a tech firm in the U.K., emphasizes the instrumental role that women in leadership can play in guiding and uniting teams. Adriana articulates, "Our influence as women in positions of authority is magnified when we serve as navigators, helping our teams discern what may not be immediately apparent to them. By clearly communicating a unified vision, we create a framework that not only aligns expectations but also empowers each member to contribute meaningfully."

The Profound Impact of Silence and Voice

It was in the shadows of a closet that young Damian learned the indelible power of silence, the raw energy of restraint. As he was pulled into the dark by his sister, he heard his mother absorbing the blows from his father. She was the epitome of resilient silence, a woman conditioned by the world around her to suppress her voice.

But life has its way of bringing enlightenment. In an era when divorces were stigmatized, Damian's mother declared her "greatest achievement" as securing her freedom. The room's laughter could not muffle her triumphant liberation. For Damian, this was a testament to the strength it takes to maintain composure even when the world is screaming at you to break.

Years later, Damian would learn another lesson from his mother, one that instilled in him a moral urgency. It was the story of her illegal border crossing, of a young boy beaten by an agent, and of a woman—just one woman—whose voice resonated loud enough to save him. Damian realized the cost of silence, the imperative need for voice.

His mother's life became a curriculum in courage. "Women bring accountability, respect, and standards to society," Damian says. "I unconsciously aspire to be my mom. She found her voice, a voice missing from her era, a voice that should've been there all along."

In the unfolding narratives of women who have found their voice, we see a common thread: the audacity to stand up, speak out, and challenge the status quo. These are not just stories; they are manifestos for change, blueprints for the next generation of women leaders.

As you venture into the world with your newly polished skills and heightened emotional intelligence, remember Damian's mother. Remember the woman who faced adversity with silence but found her voice when it mattered most. Remember that your voice is not just a set of vocal cords; it's a legacy in the making.

Harness your 'Superpower', find your voice, and let it echo through the generations. For when you speak, you don't just resonate within the walls of your life—you ripple through the universe, affecting transformative change.

Your voice is your legacy. Make it heard.

Questioning the Voice and Finding Answers

Exercising one's voice is a critical aspect of effective communication. Yet, it's equally important to understand why we should confidently use our voice. Conservation journalist, author, and entrepreneur, Ashlan Cousteau, provides a poignant illustration of this journey of understanding.

Growing up in the South, she often found herself questioning her instinct to voice her thoughts and stand her ground.

"I still find myself questioning myself. Is that a good thing to be saying? Should I stand up and say that? I was brought up to apologize for everything. That I need to be nice. But how do you find that balance and determine when you need to stand your ground?"

In her work life, she didn't have any female role

models or mentors. "There just weren't many female bosses. But when there were, it was harder for them. It's not like the corporate world had open arms to women in leadership. They had to fight to get there."

Despite lacking female mentors in her career, Ashlan credits her resilience to her strong 'tribe' of female support. The journey wasn't straightforward, though; she found motivation from unexpected sources, including a challenging mentor, Dr. Charlie Tuggle, Dr. T to students at University of North Carolina at Chapel Hill School of Journalism.

Dr. Tuggle's relentless push backs fueled Ashlan's tenacity. His faith in her, paradoxically, served as her driving force. Even amidst doubts and hardship, her strong-willed 'tribe' and her relentless spirit spurred her forward.

Ashlan's story is not only one of resilience but also a testament to the power of living a purposeful life. This realization led her to abandon her entertainment career to pursue her passion for conservation journalism. Her pivot was a testament to the incredible strength that can be found in a life guided by purpose.

Despite the societal stigma around women being 'too emotional,' Ashlan suggests that leading with heart is our unique strength as women. "Some see this as a weakness, but I see it as a strength," she asserts. She credits her tribe for boosting her confidence and supporting her decisions, even when she decided to join her husband's family's conservation legacy.

Navigating her new path wasn't smooth sailing. Doubts clouded her confidence. How would an *E-News girl* fit into a family committed to saving the planet for three generations? Yet, it was in one of her moments of self-doubt that she had a significant breakthrough: She realized the popular series 'Undersea World of Jacques Cousteau' was essentially a reality TV show.

Ashlan recalls the moment. I thought, "What was the Undersea World of Jacques Cousteau?" And then the answer came to her. The answer was obvious. She jokes, "It was the first reality television show. It was tan French men in teeny weeny bikinis, drinking wine, smoking and problem-solving. Heck! I can do that!"

It was the answer that Ashlan had been searching for. Her place. Where she could contribute and help make her husband's work look cool. Most importantly, she was following her heart and that felt amazing.

Inspired, Ashlan authored 'Oceans for Dummies,' a book series that made conservation more accessible to the layperson. She had found her niche - her unique space to contribute to the legacy she'd married into. Ashlan understood that the key was not to be loud just for the sake of it, but to speak passionately from the heart. It was through this passion that her voice gained confidence, and her leadership could truly thrive.

Her advice for the younger generation? Don't be afraid to follow your heart. Even if you aren't in your dream job. Use your skill set to make it work and bridge the gap. Use that as an opportunity to bring everyone else up. The only way to do that is to find a way to do what you love. It's important to not get so hung up on how you are going to do it. Stop worrying. Focus on what being happy could look like. That's how you change things. That's how you make a difference. It stems from your passion and your happiness.

Finally, Ashlan acknowledges the vital role that women's voices play in system thinking - a quality that propels society's betterment. Women, she argues, are continuously seeking ways to improve systems for the greater good. As women find, understand and exercise their voices, they bolster this collective strength, forming an unbreakable tribe ready to tackle any adversity head-on."

Empowering Mindsets

An Unyielding Journey

Raised amidst integrity and self-reliance, Dr. Aderonke Adejuyigbe's life story is an ode to perseverance, self-belief, and an unwavering commitment to personal values. Born in Dallas, Texas, but raised in Nigeria from the age of four, Aderonke is the child of a highly distinguished professor, a revered political leader, and a successful businesswoman. Her journey back to the United States for higher education, culminating in a doctorate degree, and her commitment to empowering young women is a testament to her resilient mindset.

Aderonke's father, known as the "Godfather of clean politics" in Nigeria for his unwavering integrity, served as the Honorable Commissioner for Health and was a consultant advisor to several politicians. Despite his high-ranking position, he was a humble and grounded individual, values he passed on to his children. Aderonke recalls him often driving them to school, in spite of the need for secret service protection. His aim was to keep the family connected, grounded, and away from the allure of the "flashy things." His mindset of integrity remains deeply rooted within Aderonke.

Her mother, a successful businesswoman owning a pharmacy and the only surviving child of seven siblings, was a beacon of resilience. Despite societal norms, she retired early to care for her disabled daughter, refusing to let her be ostracized. From her mother, Aderonke learned the importance of determination, compassion, and valuing the individual.

Aderonke returned to the United States in 1992 to pursue her education, earning undergraduate degrees in business management and administration, following a Master's in counseling and a doctorate in health administration. She attributes her unwavering commitment to finishing what she starts to her parent's teachings, and believes this is a crucial lesson for her own children. Aderonke is also a tireless advocate for people with disabilities, an expert, and leader in the field of intellectual and developmental disabilities.

Her message to young women is unequivocal and powerful: "You are beautiful and you are intelligent. Self-care is the most important thing. Know who you are. Know your philosophy. Stick to your vision. Nobody gets to decide that for you." She demonstrates this belief not just through her words but also through her actions. She founded a bible study group at her daughter's school, aimed at empowering 14 girls and their mothers to find value in their identity, combating societal pressures to people please at the expense of personal values and identity.

Dr. Adejuyigbe believes that women's contributions to society and business are marked by high levels of emotional intelligence, empathy, compassion, and effective communication. Aderonke's ability to successfully manage a substantial staff of approximately 25 plus individuals is attributed to these qualities. Her focus is on valuing and respecting each individual, emphasizing their strengths rather than focusing on weaknesses, which she believes propels everyone forward.

Her commitment to self-respect, empowerment, and community service extends beyond her workplace and family, as evidenced by her involvement in Rotary. Aderonke's story is a testament to the transformative power of empowering mindsets. She serves as a shining example for young women to follow their vision, prioritize self-care, and respect themselves and others, demonstrating that these are the foundations of strong, impactful leadership.

A Legacy of Resilience and Communication

Born to a German immigrant mother who had survived multiple World War II bombing raids, Terry Miller-Herringer learned early on the importance of determination and courage. Her mother's refusal to be limited by her muscular dystrophy diagnosis and her father's 2-year battle and eventual death from leukemia when Terry was just nine years old left indelible impressions on her young mind. In the face of adversity, Terry found strength, inspiration, and the first echoes of resilience that would shape her future.

Communication and Empathy

Building Bridges

As an adjunct faculty with the psychology department at a university in northern California, Terry's professional journey was influenced by strong male role models and mentors. This experience shaped her progressive feminist stance, where she recognized that both men and women must be held up in society to progress. Her approach to communication was guided by empathy and an understanding that balance, rather than competition, leads to healthier dialogue and collaboration.

Finding Her Voice

Pivotal Influences

Terry's belief in her own potential was awakened by a female counselor at Cal State LA. This brief but profound encouragement led her to pursue a PhD in Psychology. Two women in particular, her aunt Hazel, an elegant, powerful role model, and Sandee, a supportive colleague and co-author on a book project, further nurtured Terry's professional confidence. Through their support and her own resolve, Terry found her voice and her calling.

In navigating her academic journey, Terry's growth was marked by intense mentoring relationships, innovative research, and an unyielding desire to explore and understand. Her undergraduate and graduate mentors (many of them males), coupled with the diverse research projects she pursued, contributed to her holistic perspective on communication and leadership.

Terry's observations on the culture of pitting women against each other and the negative impact of social media on self-esteem offer a critical reflection of our times. Her insistence on being a gatekeeper of one's own self-perception, focusing on inner strengths rather than physical beauty and popularity, resonates with the lessons laid out by Patterson, Grenny, McMillan, and Switzler in Crucial Conversations: Tools for Talking When Stakes are High.

Terry's commitment to positive psychology, mindfulness meditation, and self-regulation of emotions forms the core of her philosophy. She believes in the power of asking for help, the importance of making and learning from mistakes, and the value of resilience and assertiveness. In these principles, we find echoes of what it means to harness emotional intelligence as a 'Superpower.'

An advocate for collaboration, gender equality, and practical decision-making, Terry sees women's ability to look at the bigger picture as a unique and valuable attribute. Her insights into parenting, the perils of perfectionism, and imposter syndrome offer a blueprint for a more inclusive and empathetic society, where nurturing and leadership are celebrated equally across genders.

If Terry had a magic wand, she would wish for children to find their emotional/spiritual center, for society to recognize the challenges of child-rearing on women, and for everyone to be free to pursue careers regardless of gender roles. Her vision of a world where empathy, compassion, and practicality are recognized and rewarded paints a hopeful picture for the future.

Terry Miller-Herringer's story is a rich tapestry of resilience, empathy, and empowerment. Her life's journey, marked by personal triumphs, professional achievements, and thoughtful insights, offers a unique perspective on the art of communication and negotiation. Her voice, shaped by adversity, mentors, self-reflection, and a deep understanding of human nature, resonates as an inspiring example of powerful communication.

Her legacy stands as a testament to what women can achieve through resilience, empathy, and a willingness to listen, learn, and lead. Terry's story is not just a personal narrative; it's a universal call to action, urging us to find our voice, to be gatekeepers of our own destiny, and to effect transformative change. It's a reminder that our strength lies in our practicality, our collaboration, and our unique ability to see the bigger picture. In Terry's world, every voice matters, and every voice can make a difference.

To Whom Much Is Given, Much Is Required

A Journey to Spiritual Leadership

Since the beginning of time, our belief in an omnipotent and benevolent power has been an integral part of our lives. In a world often driven by material pursuits, spiritual leadership extends beyond the tangible and visible, tapping into the intangible realms of meaning and interconnectedness. Our spiritual leaders serve as a guiding light, illuminating a path of compassion, self-discovery, and collective well-being. They transcend conventional notions of authority and tap into a profound connection to higher principles and deep understanding of our human spirit to connect and serve something greater that promotes the common good.

Chiraphone Khamphouvong's life story delves into the intricacies of spiritual leadership and unravels a tapestry of insights and the profound impact it has on both our personal and collective everyday lives.

Chiraphone was born in Sayaboury, a small village in Lao People's Democratic Republic (PDR) of Southeast Asia. Her Sanskrit name, Chiraphone, was given to her by her father's Buddhist monk teacher and means eternal and everlasting blessings.

During the civil war, when the Communist Party was gaining power, her family made the perilous escape to Thailand and lived as refugees before eventually migrating to the United States. It was during her time at the refugee camp, where the Christian missionaries introduced her to *"Pra-Yesu"* the Sanskrit name for God the Jesus and her journey to spiritual leadership began. Although many in the refugee camp immediately embraced the teachings, converted from Buddhism to Christianity and became missionaries, for Chiraphone, to be Lao is to be Buddhist, and it took her a little longer for the teachings of *Pra-Yesu* to fully resonate in her heart.

Freedom to Be...

When Chiraphone was ten she realized she had a different temperament from her siblings regarding her cultural background. With the assistance and support of their sponsors her family settled in the United States where she had her first experience of humanitarian grace of strangers being kind to strangers. This unconditional grace that was extended to her family stirred her deep within and she knew she was becoming a new person with different values than her cultural upbringing. She struggled with the new strong spiritual leaning and feelings of dishonoring her parents, especially her mother. To honor her mom, Chiraphone tried to set aside these feelings and decided to dedicate herself to becoming the best Asian daughter everyone expected. Within two weeks, her new behavior was strikingly noticeable to her mother.

"What are you doing?" asked Chiraphone's mother.

"I'm being the Asian daughter you would like and want," she responded.

"That may be the Asian daughter for others, but it's not for you."

Chiraphone can recall the feeling of that moment. "This is the moment that gave me freedom to be..." From here I had the emotional and spiritual support I needed to realize my freedom and who I was meant to be. After that it didn't take me long to embrace who I was meant to be. My classmates said I took charge or led the way with class or different programs at school. I was propelled to participate in student government, play soccer, and generally explore different opportunities.

At the age of 15, her journey to spiritual leadership truly manifested. At a Christian summer camp in California, Chiraphone met a guest speaker who foretold that God's life purpose and calling for her was "to meet the physical and spiritual needs of the people in this world" It was the supernatural moment that changed the trajectory of her life.

Chiraphone went on to graduate from Azusa Pacific University where she met more women, who she lovingly refers to as "mammas", who poured into her spiritual leadership role. She became very intentional about her leadership development and focused primarily on the spiritual call of service to others who had local, national, and international needs. After graduating, she went on to serve in the Peace Corps.

Next, realizing the Cambodian people are still in the process of healing from past regimes, Chiraphone came full circle and returned to her homeland to give back. She launched Impact Beyond Borders, a grassroots movement of strategic development approaches with Lao PDR's education, heritage, and service opportunities. Since 2022, she works as a program advisor with World Renew which focuses on rural sustainable livelihood development for the Cambodian people.

Chiraphone's message to young women exemplifies her spiritual leadership. "Be true, self-aware, and mindful of others. Don't let tribalism hold you back. The more you can give or serve others is impactful. Giving of yourself makes this world a better place. Have the freedom to BE. May the Kingdom of God be sought and found locally and internationally as a testament of God's love for each of us – where much has been given, mush is required. (Luke 12:48)."

Taking Action

Strategies for Empowering Powerful Communication

Be Brave, Be Vocal

Inspired by Ashlan's courage, don't hesitate to speak up in situations where your voice matters. Whether you're in a meeting, classroom, or a social setting, let your voice be heard. The first step to effective communication is mustering the courage to use your voice, just as Ashlan did when tackling demanding projects.

Role-Playing Exercises

Role-playing exercises can be very effective for practicing communication and negotiation skills. These exercises can simulate high-stakes negotiations or difficult conversations. Immediate feedback and repetition help identify strengths and weaknesses in your communication style.

Active Listening Techniques

Active listening is as crucial as speaking clearly. Techniques for active listening include paraphrasing, summarizing points, and asking open-ended questions. Implement these methods in your daily conversations to improve both your understanding and engagement with others.

Public Speaking Opportunities

Public speaking is a valuable skill that can greatly enhance your ability to communicate effectively. Seek opportunities to express your thoughts and ideas in front of an audience. This could mean giving a presentation at work, joining Toastmasters, or taking public speaking workshops.

Emotional Intelligence Training

Mastering your emotions is a key element in effective communication. Emotional intelligence training can help you recognize, understand, and manage your emotions and those of others. This is especially crucial for high-stakes or emotionally-charged situations.

Leverage Humility to Connect

Taking a leaf from Aderonke's book, use humility as a tool to make genuine connections. Practice empathetic communication by understanding that every person's perspective is valuable, which will not only help you learn but will also make others more receptive to your ideas.

Build a Supportive Network

Your network can significantly empower your voice and improve your communication skills. Following Ashlan's example, create your 'tribe' of supportive individuals like mentors, colleagues, and friends to provide a secure space for expressing your ideas and getting constructive feedback. From Chiraphone's spiritual leadership perspective, as mentors and leaders pour into your lives, you should invest in other lives within your sphere of influence.

Read and Learn

Expand your communication toolkit through constant learning. Consider reading books like 'Crucial Conversations: Tools for Talking When Stakes are High' and attending related webinars and courses.

Self-Reflection

Make it a habit to review and reflect on your interactions. Evaluate what went well and what could be improved, and make necessary adjustments. Like Terry, consider keeping a journal for deeper self-analysis and growth. Personal practices such as prayer and other spiritual practices also help you with self reflection and becoming more self aware.

Practice Respectful Disagreement

As illuminated by Gabriela Torres, the crux of productive conversations doesn't always lie in reaching unanimous agreement. Rather, it is in the manner in which disagreements are handled that the true tone of a conversation is set. By articulating your own viewpoints with grace and affording the space for the other party to share theirs, you foster a climate ripe for meaningful dialogue and mutual growth.

Create a Shared Vision

Drawing on Adriana Malone's insights, and Chiraphone Khamphouvong's spiritual guidings, the power of leadership extends beyond mere decision-making; it lies in the ability to shape and articulate a shared vision.

Such a vision becomes the North Star for a team, illuminating the path ahead and fostering alignment among its members.

Whether you are at the helm or a crucial part of the team, striving to articulate and share a coherent vision is imperative.

This acts as a fundamental guidepost for communications and decision-making, ensuring that everyone is not just on the same page, but also invested in achieving a common goal.

Key Takeaways

- **Courage as a Communication Tool:** Ashlan's story teaches us that bravery is the first step in making your voice heard. Her courage wasn't just physical but also about being bold enough to express her ideas.

- **Voice as a Community Instrument:** Aderonke's approach to community change reflects the need for listening as a form of powerful communication. Your voice is not just for you; it's a tool for your community.

- **Emotionally Intelligent Communication:** As Terry has shown, the key to effective communication often lies in not just what is being said, but how it's emotionally framed.

- **Strategic Silence:** Aderonke's discernment on when to speak teaches us that sometimes silence can be as powerful as words in a conversation.

- **Leverage Peer Learning:** Terry's story underscores the importance of mutual growth. Sometimes the best insights come from horizontal, not just vertical, relationships.

- **The Power of Context:** Learning from Ashlan and Aderonke, tailor your message and approach to the specific audience or situation for maximum impact.

- **Invest in Skill-building:** Both Terry and Ashlan didn't just rely on their natural talents; they invested in honing their communication skills, a necessary commitment for anyone looking to lead.

CHAPTER 4

THE POWER OF THE NETWORK

Unveiling the Tapestry of Connectedness

"In the garden of unity, every flower is unique but connected through the same soil and sun. This is the same beauty we witness in a network - each person is unique but interwoven through shared experiences, ambitions, and growth." As we embark on the exploration of Chapter 4, let's ponder upon these words and their profound resonance in our lives.

The title of this chapter, "The Power of the Network," symbolizes an essential cornerstone of human progress and evolution - interconnectedness. The story of human civilization is, in many ways, the story of networking. It's about the power of shared wisdom, collective strength, and the synergy of connections.

Just as diverse flowers constitute a garden, individuals make up the network that fuels our collective growth. Each one of us, with our unique attributes and aspirations, contributes to this intricate web of interconnectedness, drawing from and adding to the reservoir of shared wisdom. As we delve into "The Power of the Network," let's cherish this beautiful metaphor of unity, and recognize the critical role we all play in this grand tapestry of human collaboration. Together, we hold the potential to influence change, inspire innovation, and foster an environment conducive to growth for us all.

Catalyzing Change Through Collective Strength

The Transformative Power of Women's Networks

Mindy Ackermann, a force to be reckoned with, has been blazing trails in the utility industry and in the world of motorcycling. A Senior Resource Analyst by profession and a motorcycle racer by passion, she hails from sunny Southern California. When not navigating through the intricacies of energy analysis, you'll find her on the open road, mentoring other women in the thrill of the race.

Mindy's upbringing was marked by strength, resilience, and unity. In a family of women who had experienced the trials of divorce, a unique bond was forged. They acted as a tight-knit tribe, proving that in unity, there was power. "They taught all of us girls that you can do anything on your own," she fondly recalls. She watched as the women in her family tackled any task that came their way, from mowing the lawn to building a fence. This sense of independence and determination was etched into Mindy's character at a young age.

In this familial matriarchy, her grandfather played a

pivotal role, believing wholeheartedly in her abilities. "He'd crash and burn right next to me. He provided the most amazing encouragement," Mindy reminisces. His influence, coupled with the unwavering support from the women in her family, taught her a valuable lesson – there's nothing she can't do.

Her career gave her ample opportunities to apply these life lessons. One memorable instance was when her former supervisor, Roy, pushed her to present a significant project to a regional utility industry group. Public speaking was far from her comfort zone, yet Roy believed in her potential. "I was terrified! My voice was shaking and with just two minutes to go I accidentally disconnected from the virtual meeting. Roy finished the presentation, while giving me full credit for the project," she recalls. It was a pivotal moment that highlighted the importance of reputation, growth, and the power of a supportive network.

The lesson, Mindy would share with younger women, is that your reputation sticks with you. She advises them to consciously protect it. Moreover, she encourages them to remember that nothing is impossible if they're willing to put in the work. "There's never something that you can't do," she states with conviction, drawing from her personal experiences.

Mindy sees a unique "secret sauce" in the camaraderie among women. She paints a vivid picture of the magical bond that can exist among them. Regardless of the context, whether it be a women's softball team or a biking group, when women let down their guards, it fosters a comfort zone. It's a safe space to express vulnerabilities, share laughs, and seek support. This bond was epitomized in her all-women biker group when they came together to comfort a fellow biker who'd dropped her bike on her way to meet the girls. Upon sensing her embarrassment and frustration, each woman in the group, in turn spoke up about a time they too had bumbled. Each shared their embarrassing bike drop stories, met with smiles, support and laughter. "You just wouldn't have that in a co-ed group."

Women bikers are a minority at the track; out of a hundred participants, usually only two or three are women. This disparity heightens the need for support. In Mindy's eyes, this powerful network of women is crucial in the world of biking, given the distinct safety considerations for women.

Mindy also appreciates women's generally contemplative nature and their ability to view problems holistically. She aspires for a world where archaic societal norms that demean women based on gender are eradicated, allowing everyone to tap into their full potential. A woman of action and determination, Mindy Ackermann, through her experiences and insights, exemplifies the power of a supportive network, showing how it can help break barriers, build resilience, and inspire change.

Developing Connectedness

"Individually, we are one drop. Together, we are an ocean."

- Ryunosuke Satoro

This quote beautifully encapsulates the power of a network. A network, with its ability to bring diverse individuals together, transforms the isolated drops into an unstoppable wave of change. The story of Maria Pimienta, the Assistant Superintendent of Schools K-12 and the head of Human Resources in Los Angeles, CA, provides us with a striking illustration of the power of networks in leadership.

Maria's journey did not originate from a well-connected background or privileged upbringing. Rather, it was fueled by her resilience, her thirst for learning, and the powerful network she painstakingly built over the years. This network wasn't just about career advancement - it was about gaining perspectives, challenging norms, embracing diversity, and fostering a culture of mutual support and empowerment.

Early in her career, Maria recognized the value of guidance from seasoned professionals and sought mentors who could provide her with invaluable insights. This proactive approach to mentorship underscores the first strategy to building a robust network - don't be afraid to ask. Maria points out that "There seems to be a lot of 'boys causes' out there. Meaning, they help each other out, have each others' back and support each other." We need to be doing that, and it all starts with asking for help.

"Don't be afraid to ask people to be your mentor. Initiate those conversations," Maria asserts.

"Women know how to get the jobs, but they don't always know how to find their voice," Maria adds. A mentor can help bridge the learning curve by providing guidance, opening doors, and offering invaluable advice borne from their experiences. They challenge us, inspire us, and often see our potential before we can fully grasp it ourselves. "I want to learn from their knowledge, their experiences, or their mistakes, so that I don't have to."

Mentors do not hand out the keys to the kingdom, they guide, challenge, and push individuals out of their comfort zone. It's tough love at its finest. Maria credits her being mentored and having the courage to ask to be mentored with her success, but her success does not stop with where she is. Continually seeking knowledge and embracing a growth mindset, Maria asserts that there is power in numbers and how networking provides opportunities for growth and success.

Strategic Alliances and Sponsorship

Emphasizing the role of others, including her peers, Maria says that these types of alliances demonstrate the importance of lateral relationships in addition to those that may be hierarchical. This vital networking strategy - creating strategic alliances across different roles and sectors is how Maria empowers herself and increases her confidence.

Offering fresh perspectives, these relationships can provide emotional support and present opportunities for collaboration. They can help us see beyond our immediate purview and appreciate the broader impact of our actions. As Maria points out, women are often fearful of pursuing what they want. Whether a raise, a job opportunity, or simply more than they currently have, women tend to fearfully ask, "What if I fail?" The question truly should be, "What if you don't?" This is where strategic alliances come into play.

Having a support network of all levels can help with the immense pressure imposed on women. Maria notes how many of her female students feel intimidated by disillusions of 'the real world' from social networks, influencers, and shows like "Selling Sunsets". "We get caught up thinking there is something wrong with us because we aren't killing it and aren't like them." Women seeking out other women for support through strategic alliances is the solution to cutting through the illusions and keeping it real by having real conversations, working through real challenges and accepting that life sometimes throws us curve balls and together we can handle that.

Beyond mentorship, another great strategic alliance is sponsorship. Sponsors can leverage their influence to advocate for us, help move obstacles and lead us towards doors we did not know exist. Both my Ennette and I can unequivocally say that without a business sponsor we would not have been able to avail ourselves to many of our greatest career opportunities, this includes my current career status as CEO and founder of two corporations and Ennette's opportunity to run for a political office and work for several prestigious universities. It cannot be emphasized strongly enough, the importance of sponsors in providing opportunities and promoting our abilities to others. It does indeed take a village to grow, thrive and succeed.

Fostering Collaboration and Inclusivity

Maria's journey to leadership instilled in her the realization that leadership isn't merely about personal victories. A true leader empowers others to thrive. Inclusion and collaboration form the core of her leadership approach, creating a diverse, empowered network where every voice is heard. As she carried with her the lessons from her journey, this understanding became even more evident. A leader's personal success is in the success of others and helping them find and use their voice. Promoting collaboration and inclusivity in her organization is one of the ways Maria embodies this. By doing so, she's strengthening her network, making it more diverse, and cultivating a space where everyone's voices can be heard.

Gaining Confidence through Networks

Maria believes that one of the most significant barriers many women face is a lack of confidence. This is where a strong network can be a powerful tool. A network provides us with a platform to learn, make mistakes, and grow.

Actively seeking feedback and advice from our network can boost our confidence. Surrounding ourselves with individuals who believe in our abilities, and investing time and energy in building these relationships, can help us overcome self-doubt.

Maria recognizes that confidence, or lack thereof, is a crucial factor in women's career trajectories. Here, the strength of a network shines as it becomes a safe space for learning, growth, and overcoming self-doubt. In the end, remember that the essence of networking isn't about what we can get from others, but what we can give. Genuine, reciprocal relationships form the bedrock of a strong network.

Networking isn't just about gaining—it's about giving. Just as Maria lifted others on her journey, so should each of us contribute to our networks. A vibrant network is grounded in reciprocal relationships and becomes a cornerstone of the leadership journey.

Your Network is Your Net Worth

The potency of a robust network lies in its capacity to propel us into uncharted territories, providing a safety net during setbacks and fostering continuous learning and growth. Networking isn't a single event—it's an ongoing process of relationship-building. In other words, your network is your net worth.

As we dive into this ocean of opportunities that networking provides, we need to seek mentorship, establish alliances, champion inclusivity, and build confidence. Above all, we need to empower others and allow ourselves to be empowered.

The network's power is ready to be harnessed—are

you ready to step up and grasp it? After all, the charge for change lies not in the hands of the few, but in the powerful and connected many. The power is in your hands. The question is, are you ready to harness it?

Rising Through the Network

Angela Pierce's rise to becoming the CEO of a thriving tech startup is not a conventional rags-to-riches story. It's a testament to the potent power of networking and the value of persistence. Born into a modest family and raised by a single, hardworking mother, Angela was always motivated to chart her own path.

"I remember growing up in a small town, and the limited perspectives it offered. My mom was my beacon of strength and she instilled a relentless drive in me to pursue my dreams," Angela recalls.

Despite the obstacles she faced as the first person in her family to attend college, Angela was undeterred. She was a young woman with ambition, eager to break into the male-dominated tech industry.

"When I first stepped into the tech world, it was incredibly isolating," Angela shares, "But instead of feeling defeated, I saw it as an opportunity to create a network that could guide me."

Understanding the importance of mentorship,

Angela reached out to professionals in her field, joined networking events, and even sought membership in professional organizations. "I knew I couldn't walk this path alone. So, I sought out those who had paved the way before me," Angela says.

This led her to Dr. Lisa, a renowned woman in computer science. Angela fondly recalls, "Lisa was more than a mentor. She was my beacon in the often foggy path that the tech industry was for a young woman like me."

Alongside the crucial mentor-mentee relationship, Angela understood the significance of lateral relationships in her professional life. "It wasn't just about looking up for guidance; it was also about looking around. My peers had so much to offer, and their perspectives helped me grow," she asserts.

Jennifer, a seasoned executive in the tech industry, became a pivotal figure in Angela's journey. "Jennifer was my sponsor. She saw my potential when I was still grappling with self-doubt. She used her influence to pave my way, to open doors I didn't even know existed," Angela shares with gratitude.

As Angela rose through the ranks, she carried the lessons of her journey with her. She believed in fostering an inclusive environment and promoting a collaborative culture. "My leadership approach is rooted in empowering others," she explains. "I learned that a leader's success is tied to the success of their team, and I wanted to create a space where everyone's voice is heard."

Angela's network not only opened doors for her but also played a crucial role in her personal growth. "The reassurances, feedback, and opportunities for collaboration that I received from my network boosted my confidence," she shares. "I wasn't afraid to make mistakes because I knew I was in a safe space."

Today, Angela is keen to give back to her network, as she mentors young women making their first steps in the tech industry. "I see myself in these young women, and I know the challenges they face. I want to be the mentor I had in Lisa and the sponsor I had in Jennifer," she states passionately.

Angela's journey is a powerful demonstration of how a robust professional network can propel one's career. Her story serves as a reminder that your network truly is your net worth, and that networking isn't just about taking - it's also about giving back. In Angela's words, "I wouldn't be where I am today without my network. It's about giving and receiving in equal measure. My journey is not just about me - it's about all the individuals who have been a part of it."

Building a Beacon of Hope

Beatrice, a retired elementary school teacher, transformed her local community with her vision and the power of her network. With grit, passion, and the strength of her connections, she started a food pantry at her local church, impacting thousands of lives.

"I never imagined I'd run a food pantry in my retirement," Beatrice confessed, "But seeing the growing needs of my community, I knew I had to do something."

Beatrice was not a woman of vast resources, but she was rich in relationships. She had a lifetime of connections from her teaching career and her active role in the community, and she realized the potential of this network to make a difference.

"When I first had the idea, I didn't know where to start," she admitted. "But I knew I had a network of individuals who might help - former colleagues, parents, local business owners, even my book club friends."

Beatrice began reaching out to her connections, sharing her vision and asking for their support. To her surprise, the response was overwhelming. People volunteered their time, donated food, and used their own networks to raise awareness.

One of her former students, Rachel, a reporter at a

local news channel, played a pivotal role. "Rachel helped me get the word out about the pantry, and suddenly, donations started pouring in," Beatrice explained.

Along with financial and material donations, Beatrice's network provided invaluable moral support and guidance. Her friend, Margaret, who had experience in nonprofit management, provided insights and mentorship. "Margaret was my guide in navigating through the logistical challenges. I was a teacher, not a businesswoman, and her expertise was a godsend."

As the food pantry began to take shape, Beatrice recognized the importance of fostering a collaborative and inclusive environment. She created a diverse team of volunteers from different backgrounds and ages, drawing on the strength of her network.

"The food pantry was not just about me. It was about our community coming together," Beatrice states. "It was about empowering each other, and lifting each other up."

Running the food pantry not only impacted her community but also helped Beatrice grow personally. "I learned so much about leadership, about kindness, about resilience," she shares. "The journey gave me confidence, it gave me purpose, and it reminded me of the power of connections."

Today, Beatrice's food pantry serves hundreds of

families each week. More than that, it has become a symbol of unity and compassion in her community.

"I couldn't have done this alone," Beatrice reflects. "My network was my lifeline. It was my safety net. It gave me the courage to dream and the resources to turn those dreams into reality."

Beatrice's journey is a testament to the incredible power of networking. Her story serves as a reminder that our networks are not just about career advancement or personal gain. They can also be harnessed to create lasting, meaningful change in our communities. In Beatrice's words, "We all have a network. The question is, how are we using it to make a difference?"

Taking Action

Strategies for Incorporating Networking for Leadership Skill Building

Incorporate Networking in Daily Life

Much like Beatrice, recognize that your existing community connections can become the building blocks for change. Don't wait for networking events; start by reaching out to people in your current circles.

Share Your Vision

As Beatrice did, don't hesitate to communicate your

vision or cause when you network. Whether it's a club meeting or an industry event, speaking about your purpose can attract like-minded individuals.

Utilize Social Media Mindfully

Beyond connecting with professionals, use platforms like LinkedIn to share articles and thoughts that resonate with your vision or cause. This will not only make you visible but also attract people who align with your values.

Be Open to Mentorship and Sponsorship

Much like Maria and Angela, seek out relationships that offer more than just career advice. Look for mentors and sponsors who can help you grow personally and contribute to your community.

Collaborate for a Cause

Initiate or participate in projects that align with your interests and can bring about community change. Collaborations not only enhance your network but also help you grow in your leadership journey, much like Beatrice's food pantry did.

Keep in Touch for the Long Haul

Take a leaf out of Beatrice's book and maintain connections not for immediate gain but for long-term

DR. JOLENE CHURCH & DR. ENNETTE MORTON

relationships. Check in with people in your network periodically, even if it's just to say hello.

Leverage Professional Organizations for Community Impact

Being part of professional organizations or clubs like Toastmasters is not just about your professional growth; use this platform to create projects that impact your community positively.

Think Inclusively

When building your network, ensure it's diverse. A varied network provides a rich ecosystem for not just career growth, but also personal and community development.

Invest in Skill-Sharing and Learning

Dedicate some time each month to either teach something you are good at or learn from someone in your network. It's a two-way street that fosters a strong, interconnected community.

Reflect and Refresh

Every six months, take stock of your network's health. Are you giving as much as you are receiving? Is the network aligned with your current goals? Pivot or diversify as needed.

Key Takeaways

- **Your Network is Your Net Worth:** As seen from Beatrice's story, your network is more than just a career ladder; it can be a lifeline in personal and community-based endeavors.

- **Diverse Networks Foster Resilient Communities:** The more varied your network, the more robust your community projects will be, much like Beatrice's food pantry.

- **Intentionality Over Volume:** It's not just about how many people you know, but how well you know them. Aim for deep, meaningful connections over a long list of acquaintances.

- **Mentors and Sponsors Serve Different but Crucial Roles:** A well-rounded network has both. Mentors guide you, while sponsors can open doors you didn't even know existed.

- **Reciprocity is Key:** Networking isn't a one-way street. The most robust networks are built on mutual support and shared values.

- **Social Capital Can Drive Social Change:** Networking isn't merely a professional tool; it can be leveraged for societal benefit.

- **Digital Networking is Not Secondary:** The importance of face-to-face connections is indisputable, but digital connections can be just as meaningful and far-reaching.

- **Networking is Skill Building:** Each interaction helps you improve your communication, negotiation, and leadership abilities.

- **Never Underestimate the Power of a Single Connection:** One meaningful relationship can be the catalyst for unprecedented growth and change, personally and community-wise.

- **Community Involvement Amplifies Networking:** Being involved in your community, be it through a food pantry or a professional organization, enhances your networking circle and adds a layer of depth to your relationships.

CHAPTER 5

WORK-LIFE BALANCE AND SELF-CARE AS ROLE MODELS FOR THE NEXT GENERATION

"When a woman stands tall, she becomes the beacon of hope that illuminates the path for others to follow."

– Malala Yousafzai

Living in a rapidly-evolving world, a culture that prizes accomplishment, productivity, and constant activity can often make it challenging for women to strike an authentic work-life balance. The societal narrative frequently presents an image of a "superwoman" who can seamlessly juggle a successful career, personal life, family responsibilities, while also maintaining her health and hobbies. This impossible standard of perfection not only raises stress levels but also clouds the richness of daily experiences.

As role models for the next generation of young women, our task extends beyond pursuing our personal work-life balance. It's vital to consciously exemplify how to value oneself, manage stress, embrace vulnerability, and enjoy the fleeting beauty of the present moment.

In this way, we can educate them about setting realistic expectations and the importance of self-care, thereby shaping a healthier, more compassionate generation of women.

Dancing the Dance

In the luminous theater of life, playing multiple roles simultaneously can sometimes be overwhelming. As a mother of four grown children and a grandmother to seven, an author, speaker, and CEO of two companies, I have danced this intricate ballet for many years. Balancing the myriad responsibilities and commitments has consistently been my most challenging act.

My wonderful husband, with his zen-like aura of "chill" and his endearing "don't worry, be happy" ethos, serves as my anchor amidst the storm.

His serenity counterbalances my dynamism, reminding me of the necessity to be intentional about self-care, maintaining balance, and staying grounded in the present.

Observing our distinct ways of functioning, I'm often struck by the beauty of our complementary roles. Our contrasting attitudes serve as an enlightening testament to the reality that there are different pathways to living a fulfilling and successful life.

It underscores the importance of seeking out and nurturing our unique balance, not dictated by societal norms, but shaped by personal well-being and happiness.

The delicate dance of life accelerates for young women who often find themselves caught in the whirlwind of being a 'superwoman.' The aspiration to excel in all aspects of life, to be an impeccable professional, a nurturing mother, a caring daughter, an unwavering support system, all while tending to their personal dreams and passions, can be an exhausting pursuit. The paradigm of the 'superwoman' often casts a shadow over the simple joys of life, moments that form the threadwork of our human existence.

The gossamer threads of time weave the moments into the rich tapestry of life, each moment as transient as it is precious. As a mother, I've felt this keenly. Time, in its relentless march forward, transforms the seemingly endless nights of caring for a sick child into fleeting memories that you hold onto dearly. These moments, although challenging at the time, are imbued with a love and tenderness that remain etched in your heart long after your children have grown.

It is this understanding that needs to be imparted to young women - the understanding that it's okay not to juggle everything perfectly. Life, with its ebbs and flows, is not about achieving perfection, but about appreciating the imperfect moments that fill our days. It's about acknowledging that it's okay to feel overwhelmed at times, to admit that you're tired, to seek help when needed, and to take a pause to breathe and just be.

The beauty of life lies in these moments of 'being.' It's in the quiet morning savored over a cup of tea, in the laughter shared over a family dinner, or in the thrill of a spontaneous adventure. The acceptance of one's own imperfections and vulnerabilities creates a conducive environment for authentic growth and equilibrium. It shifts the focus from the exhausting quest of being a 'superwoman' to the enriching journey of being a 'happy woman.'

This profound lesson forms the crux of my message to young women. By embracing imperfections and living in the moment, they can redefine their success, not as an outward display of achievements, but as an inward sense of peace, happiness, and balance. It's about enabling them to cultivate a mindful approach to life, one where they value their well-being, seek support when needed, and most importantly, savor the joy in every moment. As they navigate their path, this wisdom can serve as their guiding light, illuminating their journey towards a fulfilling and balanced life.

Embracing Self-Discovery

Born and raised in the picturesque terrains of Maine, Jennifer Oknin, a University of Maine alumna, enthusiastically launched into the corporate world. A realm filled with data-informed decision-making and dynamic leadership, it was here that Jennifer devoted herself wholeheartedly, embracing every challenge to ascend to the next executive level.

Throughout her 20s and 30s, Jennifer wholly immersed herself in the corporate whirlwind. A passionate "company girl", she championed the corporate ethos, channeling her personal ambitions and needs into her professional growth. However, life has a knack for steering us toward unanswered inquiries, and it nudged Jennifer when her career demanded her to reevaluate her priorities.

Standing at this juncture, Jennifer found herself confronted with a significant question she had long overlooked: "What does Jen want?" This question stirred a profound determination within her to regain control of her life and prioritize her ambitions. Amid the hustle of corporate life, she recognized the importance of maintaining her friendships and personal relationships, marking the start of a self-discovery journey that would shape her understanding of herself and her potential to influence others positively.

As Jennifer progressed on this journey, she realized the necessity of achieving balance in her life and mitigating the mounting stress. This epiphany was further emphasized when she prepared for an overseas onboarding assignment for international team members. Confronted with a wardrobe that no longer fit, Jennifer addressed the health implications of her high-stress lifestyle. With this acknowledgment, she took control of her wellbeing, physically challenging herself by training for a half marathon, and mentally nurturing herself. She decided to shift her focus from the corporate goals to her personal aspirations.

During this period, Jennifer was introduced to a health and wellness-based MLM business opportunity. This opportunity served as her initial toe touch into entrepreneurship, with the corporate salary as her safeguard.

As Jennifer embarked on her self-discovery journey, she questioned, "What makes me happy?" and "What does my ideal day look like?" The lure of corporate accolades no longer satisfied her. She desired something beyond where she was, yet she couldn't envision herself completely leaving the corporate world.

Jennifer found herself at a crucial turning point when the corporation she had dedicated herself to underwent significant changes, leaving her feeling marginalized. Rather than view this as a setback, Jennifer perceived it as a sign to focus on her needs. She gracefully resigned, ensuring a smooth transition for the company over two months. She looks back with pride at the mindful and respectful manner in which she closed her corporate chapter.

On the cusp of her wedding, Jennifer decided to dive completely into the realm of entrepreneurship. She admits this journey was more demanding than she had anticipated. "I've always been one to take the leap," she openly shares. The reward, however, was a newfound autonomy, the ability to control her own time, and the luxury of flexibility, such as attending a 10 am exercise class on a Monday. Life was no longer shackled to the strict nine-to-five routine. With the unwavering support of her soon-to-be husband, she was able to concentrate on her business venture without the worry of financial security. This support gave Jennifer the love and space she needed to truly "figure herself out."

Learning to prioritize her needs over pleasing others was a challenging lesson, but crucial to Jennifer's growth. She started understanding the importance of establishing her identity beyond the corporate expectations. As a leader, Jennifer believes in the "hug 'em and kick 'em" approach, a style she borrowed from a valued female mentor, emphasizing a supportive yet accountable environment. This approach allows Jennifer to guide her clients towards their maximum potential, a stark contrast from her early corporate days where she experienced intimidation.

Today, as the Founder/CEO of Shift into Health and a certified holistic health practitioner, Jennifer is a beacon of transformation. With her Fatigued to Fabulous Program, she empowers women to be the best versions of themselves, advocating for health, confidence, and energy. She promotes "listening to the whispers of your body, before they become a scream" and encourages open conversations about women's hormonal changes and their effects in the workplace.

Jennifer posits that women, in their innate ability to manage various life aspects, bring a holistic perspective to the workplace. For future generations, she encourages alignment between their personal and professional lives. "Ladies...It's an amazing feeling to love your career, your kids, your life. But you can't be so wrapped up in it all that you ignore the whispers of your body. You have to listen as it starts to tell you that you are running too hard, too fast, and are starting to pay the consequences. Get quiet with yourself, take stock, and then get into action. You are the CEO of your own life! Prioritize yourself and I promise you won't regret it!"

In an era of extremes, Jennifer Oknin underlines the importance of balance, self-care, and mental, emotional, and physical wellness. Her story is a testament to the power of self-awareness and self-love, reminding us that it's okay to prioritize ourselves and that understanding ourselves is the first step towards advocating for ourselves.

Melanie's Multifaceted Balance

Melanie, a dynamic mother of two, an enthusiastic hiker, and a thriving entrepreneur, carries a profound understanding of the delicate dance between work and life.

Her journey wasn't always straightforward, but her struggles were transformative, as they gradually molded her into a beacon for other women to look up to.

"Balance isn't something that just happens," Melanie mused. "It's an intentional act, a choice you make every day, in every situation. Some days, it means knowing when to shut off your computer and play with your kids. Other times, it's the opposite - you have to prioritize work. The key is in knowing you can't be all things to all people all the time."

Melanie's words of wisdom resonate with her experience, illuminating her mindset towards work-life balance. "Self-care isn't just bubble baths and yoga classes. It's taking the time to sit with yourself, to understand your needs, and address them - be it physical, emotional, or mental."

Sculpting Peace

Gina, a Bay Area sculptor whose art has graced the homes of the rich and famous. Gina found her unique rhythm in the dichotomy of her fast-paced artistic career and her tranquil personal life. She emphasizes the critical role of self-care, not only for personal wellness but as a model for the younger generation.

"Growing up, I watched my mother exhaust herself, trying to do it all, and I swore I would find a better way," Gina says. "I realized that, just like in sculpting, you have to carve out time for yourself, to rejuvenate and realign with your inner peace."

Gina's approach to work-life balance became a testament to her values. "There's a beautiful, undervalued strength in saying 'no' when things become too much. It's okay to rest, to take a step back and breathe. That's not a failure; it's an act of self-respect."

A Unified Approach

Uma, a tenacious high school teacher, and a single mother, became a living example of the power of mindful living and positive prioritization.

Her journey was marked by challenges, but her consistent focus on self-care and resilience inspired many of her students.

"I used to feel guilty if I took time for myself," Uma admits. "But I realized I can't pour from an empty cup. I needed to take care of myself before I could adequately care for my students or my son."

Uma's wisdom emanates from her lived experiences. "Prioritize the essentials, let go of the things that are not serving you. Value your time and ensure you dedicate some of it to doing what you love and what makes you happy. That is the foundation of true balance."

Dancing to the Rhythm of Her Soul

From the first beat of life, Jennifer Waters Howells danced to a rhythm only she could hear. Born into a family where dance wasn't just a hobby but a calling, Jennifer embraced the world with open arms, twirling in the flow of passion that had been passed down through generations.

"Dancing in the womb," as Jennifer recalls, was merely the prelude to a life that would go far beyond the dance floor. It was a metaphor for the graceful way she moved through life, intertwining the elegance of dance with the philosophy of self-love and acceptance.

A Teacher's Faith, A Student's Awakening

In the 3rd grade, Jennifer's world was expanded by a teacher who saw something extraordinary in her. Challenging her with 5th-grade math, this educator's belief in Jennifer's abilities ignited a spark of self-confidence that had never burned so brightly before. "He believed in me," Jennifer reflects, the joy of realization still fresh in her voice. "I didn't know how good I was until he helped me realize that I had a gift for math. It inspired me to keep working."

Dance, Spirituality, and Self-Discovery

Growing up, dance and spirituality wove themselves seamlessly into Jennifer's DNA. Even though raised in a Methodist church, she was drawn to the teachings of Caroline Myss and the art of yoga, finding solace in the realization that spirituality didn't have to fit into an organized religious box. The struggle with perfectionism, the silent tormentor of many a dancer, led her on a journey towards acceptance and self-love. She found her center in yoga, recognizing the spiritual beings within, dancing to the tune of daily acceptance and resilience.

Choreographing a Life of Balance

Today, as an author, choreographer, dancer, yoga instructor, and owner of Dance Big Sky in Montana,

Jennifer's philosophy shines through her words and actions. "I'm working on recovering from perfectionism, and I'm still okay." Her empathy allows her to recognize the negative energy in others—fear of failure, judgment, rejection, the torture of perfectionism. She's there to remind them, "I've been doing this my whole life. Don't be afraid to be bad at something until you aren't. Life isn't a competition."

Jennifer's words of wisdom resonate with an authenticity borne of lived experience: "You must live what makes you happy. Someone else cannot show you what your happiness is." Her advocacy for independence in choice and the unique nurturing perspective that women bring to the world empowers those she teaches.

Living in Purpose, Writing in Flow

As an author of "Marie's Dream," Jennifer allowed her inner voice to flow freely, penning a story of the importance of self-belief to the realization of dreams. It's a reflection of her life, where dance is not just an art form but an expression of her innermost self. Jennifer believes that her ability to balance, go with the flow, and be in tune with her inner truth is what defines her. "I don't desire an imbalanced life that takes me away from what I love or who I am. I am self-expression."

Jennifer Waters Howells is more than a dancer; she's

a beacon for the next generation, illuminating a path where self-care and work-life balance are not just concepts but a way of life. Her story, a dance of resilience, self-love, and empowerment, stands as a testament to the truth in Malala Yousafzai's words: "When a woman stands tall, she becomes the beacon of hope that illuminates the path for others to follow." Her legacy is a choreography of the soul, guiding others towards a life of authenticity, grace, and endless possibility.

Life's Short, Live It!

Amidst the bustling corridors and echoing classrooms of high school is where the story of Kathleen and Craig Hostert began weaving together the lives of two souls destined for each other. The two sweethearts were married in 1984 and three years into their marriage Craig was diagnosed with an autoimmune kidney disease. As the seasons changed and their journey unfolds, these two hearts navigated the uncharted path together, bound by love and a strong belief in God. During the next nine and a half years their lives would change dramatically.

Kathleen had already been four years into her teaching career when Craig's dialysis journey commenced, sparking the search for a compatible kidney donor. Observing Craig's strenuous dialysis sessions left an immense impact on the entire family. However, a turning point arrived when they crossed paths with an individual who had undergone a successful transplant; this revelation opened doors to the possibility of a related living donation, instilling newfound hope within them. Promptly each family member underwent testing to determine their compatibility as a potential donor. Unbeknownst to Craig, among those tested was Kathleen, who later discovered that she was indeed a suitable match. Following two and a half years of grappling with dialysis, Kathleen selflessly offered her kidney to Craig, granting him a remarkable second chance at life.

After providing unwavering support to Craig during years of dialysis and selflessly donating a kidney for his life-saving surgery, Kathleen underwent a profound transformation in her life's purpose. Despite her deep affection for teaching, this life-altering experience illuminated a new path for her—a mission centered around guiding, aiding, and motivating individuals in similar circumstances. Consequently, she made the difficult decision to relinquish her cherished teaching position. Collaborating with Craig, they assumed the roles of ambassadors for the transplant community and established the "Donate Life Run-Walk." Fast forward 14 years, and Craig's kidneys faced another setback. This time, his son Justin offered his kidney, giving his father another precious gift of life. The Hostert family invested boundless dedication into the growth of the Donate Life Run Walk organization, forging connections with remarkable individuals and fostering a resilient support network. As the COVID-19 pandemic swept across the globe, the Hasterts eventually retired from organizing the walk, but their indelible legacy continues to thrive.

Shortly after retiring from the "Donate Life Run-Walk," the unimaginable happened: Craig was diagnosed with cancer. In the face of this challenge, Kathleen once again turned to her unwavering faith and answered the call to help. Motivated by the incredible individuals they encountered during Craig's chemotherapy journey and the family's own experience in supporting his recovery, the concept of "Life's Short–Live It!" movement was born.

Through their website, they offer a range of inspirational apparel, with the proceeds dedicated to advancing cancer research. The fundamental objective and driving force behind the "Life's Short—Live It!" movement is to realign people with what truly matters in life through tangible reminders.

It serves as a beacon, reminding us that tomorrow might not unfold as today does, underscoring the importance of living in the present moment. Central to this philosophy is the notion that with faith, the future can hold something even better. As Kathleen and Craig celebrate the 2nd year anniversary of "Life's Short—Live it!" They are also celebrating the remarkable progress Craig has made on his journey to beat cancer.

Kathleen passionately advises women leaders to remember that life is short, and time is so precious. While juggling numerous responsibilities, it's crucial not to overlook the beauty of the journey, no matter how challenging. In the pursuit of leadership excellence, it's essential to strike a balance that enriches your life, and brings you fulfillment.

Taking Action

Strategies for Demonstrating Balance and Self-Love

Channel Your Inner Uma

Make self-care a priority. Schedule some "me time" every day to rejuvenate, even if it's just a 15-minute walk or reading a chapter from a book. Like Uma, understand that you can't pour from an empty cup.

The Dance of Life

Inspired by Jennifer Waters Howells, find an art form or hobby that makes you lose track of time. It could be painting, dancing, or even gardening. Let this hobby be your escape, your sanctuary.

Role-Model Test

Identify a role model or mentor like Jennifer's third-grade teacher. It doesn't have to be someone famous—just someone who embodies the qualities or skills you admire. Reach out to them, learn from them.

Mindful Minutes

Incorporate mindfulness techniques into your daily routine. Start with just 5 minutes a day of focused breathing or simple meditation. Grow this practice over time, much like Jennifer found her center in yoga.

The Boundary Blueprint

Develop a set of personal and professional boundaries. Practice stating these boundaries clearly and assertively, without guilt. Remember, a 'no' to something is a 'yes' to yourself.

Weekly Reflection Ritual

Establish a habit of reflecting on your week. Write down your achievements, challenges, and what you've learned. Use this reflection for setting or modifying your goals, much like the women in your guidebook have done.

Embrace Your Imperfections

Create an "It's Okay" list. On this list, jot down things that you think are imperfections or failures and reframe them as stepping stones for personal growth, embracing the power of vulnerability.

Prioritize Like Uma

Work on distinguishing between urgent and important tasks. Delegate when possible, and remember that it's alright not to do it all. Uma's journey teaches us the power of positive prioritization.

The Stress-Reduction Toolbox

Build a list of stress-reduction techniques that work for you. It could be as simple as a cup of tea, a few yoga poses, or listening to a specific playlist. When stress mounts, go to your toolbox.

Balance is the Key

Remember to balance your ambitions with self care and moments of relaxation, as a well-rounded life can lead to greater fulfillment. Embrace new experiences, learn, grow, and make the most of every opportunity that comes your way.

Debunk the Myth

We need to debunk the myth of the "perfect woman" and replace it with the image of a "real woman" who has strengths and weaknesses, who succeeds and makes mistakes, and who needs help and support from time to time. Teach them that it's okay to be imperfect, and it's okay to show vulnerability. Sharing your struggles and challenges will make them realize that setbacks are not failures but stepping stones to success.

As role models, we have the opportunity to shape the mindset of the next generation of women. By demonstrating these principles, we can help them to see that success is not just about external achievements but also about inner happiness, peace, and balance. It's about helping them understand that being a 'happy woman' who appreciates life's simple pleasures can be far more rewarding than striving to be a 'superwoman' who's always chasing societal approval. By nurturing these values, we can foster a generation that values personal well-being and creates a more compassionate, understanding society.

Key Takeaways

- **Embodying Work-Life Balance:** Just as Uma and Jennifer show us, living a balanced life enhances your well-being and sets a strong example for the next generation.

- **Redefining Perfection:** Life isn't about ticking all the boxes; it's about finding happiness in the imperfect moments and in the journey itself.

- **Cultivating Time Management and Prioritization Skills:** Learning how to manage your time and set priorities is not just for personal benefit but serves as a powerful example to others.

- **Establishing and Respecting Boundaries:** Boundaries are essential for mental health. Saying 'no' is not a sign of weakness but a declaration of self-respect.

- **Emphasizing Mindfulness and Stress Reduction:** Practicing mindfulness and stress reduction techniques enriches your life and makes you a more resilient individual.

- **Valuing Self-reflection and Personal Growth:** Regular self-reflection and goal-setting provide the blueprints for personal and professional growth.

- **Encouraging Personal Interests and Hobbies:** Hobbies are not just pastimes; they are critical for maintaining a balanced life and should be prioritized.

- **Embracing Imperfection and Vulnerability:** Authenticity and vulnerability are strengths that pave the way for deeper connections and personal growth.

- **Reimagining Success:** As Jennifer aptly says, "Life isn't a competition." Your definition of success should encompass your personal well-being and happiness, not just societal norms and expectations.

CHAPTER 6

LEADERSHIP STYLES AND STRATEGIES

"Embrace your inner warrior, for she is the fearless force that will guide you to greatness and beyond."

– Amelia Earhart

History abounds with the names of those who have led nations, transformed industries, and championed causes. The echoes of their extraordinary feats resonate in the halls of time. But leadership, in its purest form, isn't bound by grandeur or by the gilded portraits in a hallowed hall. Leadership is a flame kindled in the heart, a force that propels us forward, challenging the status quo, and charting our path into the uncharted territories of the future. In this tapestry of leaders, the threads of ordinary women shine brightly, their stories an inspirational testament to the diversity of leadership styles and strategies.

Imagine if you will, a busy hospital in the heart of a bustling city. Here, we find Dr. Susan, not merely navigating the complexities of medical practice, but shepherding her team through the stormy seas of healthcare. She is a beacon of calm amidst chaos, her leadership style founded on empathy and resilience, her strategy – a blend of decisive action and compassionate understanding.

Now, transport your mind to a school tucked away in a quiet suburb. Standing at the helm of this microcosm of society is Principal Anita. She is a relentless champion of education, her leadership echoing in the school's corridors, resonating in every learner's success. Her strategy is a unique blend of discipline and innovation, as she molds the minds that will shape tomorrow.

These stories may seem ordinary, even commonplace. But each tale is a study of leadership, a lesson in managing teams, and a masterclass in inspiring change. Each story showcases a woman who has stepped up, taken the reins, and decided not to wait for someone else to solve problems.

As we delve into this chapter, we invite you to explore the broad spectrum of leadership styles, from the transformative to the transactional, the autocratic to the laissez-faire. We aim to show you how ordinary women, just like Susan and Anita, have employed these styles effectively in their lives, crafting strategies that have allowed them to navigate challenges and triumph over adversity.

The purpose of this chapter, and indeed this book, is

to serve as your guidebook. To inspire you to harness your own leadership style, to empower you to devise your strategy, and to encourage you to step into a role of leadership. Our aim is to demonstrate, through real-world examples, that the arena of leadership is not confined to the few, but is a stage where every woman can shine.

Through the course of this chapter, let the tales of everyday women leaders inspire you. Learn from their experiences, adapt their strategies, and chart your path in leadership. Remember, leadership is not a title bestowed upon the few; it's a choice, a commitment, a journey that every woman can embark upon.

Leading with Purpose

In the tranquil ambiance of a sunny suburban school, Principal Anita marshals her institution like a seasoned ship captain navigating through both calm and stormy seas. Her leadership style is a unique blend of traditional discipline and innovative thinking, firmly rooted in respect for every individual's potential.

"In the journey of leadership," Anita says, reflecting on her experience, "there's one lesson that has always guided me. Everyone, no matter who they are, has a wealth of untapped potential inside them. As a leader, it's my job to nurture that potential, to help it grow and flourish."

Anita's path to leadership was not a straightforward one. She began her career as a classroom teacher, a role she loved for its direct impact on the lives of students. However, a growing sense of responsibility gradually propelled her towards the path of school leadership.

"I was comfortable in my classroom," she remembers, "But I realized that if I wanted to make a broader impact, I needed to step out of my comfort zone and embrace larger challenges. That was a tough decision to make. I had to let go of the familiar to embark on an entirely new journey."

Anita's wisdom rings clear in her advice for other women aspiring to leadership roles. "Courage," she says, "is a vital trait for any leader. The courage to challenge the status quo, to step outside your comfort zone, and to make difficult decisions. It is not always about making the popular decision, but about making the right one."

Anita also emphasizes the importance of empathy and emotional intelligence in leadership. "You cannot lead people effectively without understanding them, without feeling what they feel, without empathizing with their joys and their struggles. Empathy is the bridge that connects a leader to her team."

In today's fast-paced, technologically driven world, Anita underscores the importance of innovation in her leadership strategy. "We live in a dynamic world. As leaders, we need to be flexible, open-minded, and ready to adapt. We need to foster a culture of innovation, where new ideas are encouraged and failures are seen as opportunities for learning."

Perhaps the most poignant piece of advice from Anita is her take on success. "Success is not a destination," she says, "it's a journey. It's about the difference you make, the lives you touch, the legacy you leave behind. That's the true measure of leadership success."

Principal Anita's story is an inspirational testament to women's leadership. Her journey underlines the power of courage, empathy, and innovation, and offers an invaluable perspective on the essence of success. Through her words, she offers a roadmap for other women and girls looking to forge their path in leadership, one step at a time.

Leading with Empathy and Resilience

In the heart of a bustling city, amidst the constant thrum of life, stands a hospital where Dr. Susan exercises her leadership role with unwavering resilience and boundless empathy. Navigating the intricate intricacies of healthcare, she has become more than just a doctor – she is a beacon of hope and a source of inspiration for her team.

"My journey to leadership was not planned," Dr. Susan admits, "It happened organically as I felt a growing need to do more, to contribute more, to impact more lives. As a doctor, you're trained to diagnose, treat, and heal. But as a leader in healthcare, I learned that I also needed to guide, inspire, and mentor."

Dr. Susan's leadership style has evolved from her direct experiences in patient care. "The patient's wellbeing is at the core of everything we do," she says. "So, my leadership style is one that puts empathy at its center. I aim to understand, connect, and support both my patients and my team."

Even in the high-pressure environment of healthcare, Dr. Susan manages to stay resilient, a trait she considers crucial to leadership. "Resilience is not just about bouncing back," she muses, "it's about moving forward despite challenges and obstacles. It's about navigating through storms and emerging stronger on the other side."

Reflecting on her own journey, Dr. Susan has several pieces of advice for other women and girls who aspire to leadership roles. "The path to leadership can be daunting, and there will be obstacles," she says. "But don't let the fear of stumbling prevent you from walking the path. Embrace your missteps as opportunities for growth, as steps towards resilience."

Dr. Susan strongly advocates for mentorship in her leadership approach. "Seek mentors, and be a mentor," she advises. "We all need guidance, inspiration, and a safe space to grow. As a leader, you have the opportunity to provide that space for others."

She also emphasizes the need for continuous learning. "Never stop learning, never stop growing," she adds. "A leader needs to evolve with the times, adapt to new situations, and always strive for excellence. This requires an insatiable curiosity and a commitment to lifelong learning."

However, perhaps the most touching piece of advice from Dr. Susan is her view on the purpose of leadership. "Leadership isn't about power," she asserts, "it's about service. It's about making a difference in the lives of others. As you travel the road to leadership, always keep this at the forefront of your mind."

Dr. Susan's leadership story is a testament to the power of empathy, resilience, and continuous learning. Her insights offer invaluable guidance for other women and girls on their journey to leadership, illuminating the path with her own lessons learned and wisdom gained.

Redefining Leadership from a Woman's Perspective

Simone Fulmer-Gaus's story is a beacon of perseverance and innovation in the field of law, particularly in Oklahoma City, where she is a law firm owner. Her journey wasn't without its trials, but her vision and resolve have forged a new path for women in a traditionally male-dominated industry.

Raised in a community that groomed her for the roles of wife and mother, Simone's dreams were not confined to conventional expectations. She envisioned a different path, one that she carved with determination and ingenuity. Her law firm was not merely a place of business; it was a sanctuary where lawyers could grow, thrive, and avoid the ego-driven culture of other plaintiff firms.

"I built this from a woman's perspective," Simone asserts, reflecting on how her nurturing and purpose-driven approach sets her firm apart. "That type of environment that doesn't regard what their people need doesn't teach you anything," she adds, emphasizing the value of building people up.

Simone's unique vision sprouted from her experiences working in male-led firms. Though they deemed themselves "progressive," her partners were locked in an ego-driven mentality, and the pressures to conform were immense. Many female lawyers of her time were pushed to "act like a man to be taken seriously." But Simone's journey was guided by wisdom and mentorship from other great lawyers who showed her she didn't need to lose herself to succeed.

The misogynistic culture she faced was palpable, even leading her to temporarily concede to being second in charge. A socialized belief system had her doubting herself, but a revelation emerged as she approached her late 40s. "Success is not who you are second to," she realized. It was time for Simone to take charge, and at 47, she embarked on building her firm.

Her vision was not only progressive but timely. Straddling the generations of boomers and millennials, Simone understood the changing tides. Money was no longer the sole motivator; culture and lifestyle mattered. "Why not me?" she thought, seeing the void left by her male peers.

Simone's philosophy extends beyond her profession. Inspired by the teachings of Don Miguel Ruiz, she believes in forward-thinking and not living in regret. Her secret to success is rooted in these principles, along with the recognition of her own power, something she's done giving away.

Her path has been marked by various twists, from a voice/music major to teaching music, and finally pursuing law after an inspiring suggestion. Despite societal biases labeling ambition as a "dirty word" for women in her time,

Simone knew her potential. Leadership roles in student organizations hinted at her future success.

Simone credits her resilience to her father's love and belief in her, along with her mother's strength. Never afraid to seize an opportunity, Simone's approach to life is encapsulated by her sister's words: "You have always been looking around the corner for what's next."

Her advice to her younger self is poignant and universally applicable: "Figure out what you want. Don't let life happen to you." In her remarkable journey, Simone exemplifies the uncharted territories that women can explore, reshaping landscapes, and leading with purpose. Her legacy is a testament to the diversity of leadership styles, a vibrant thread in the rich tapestry of women who lead and inspire. Her story stands as a beacon, encouraging women to embrace their inner warriors, guiding them to greatness and beyond.

Leading a Life of Service

"The best way to find yourself is to lose yourself in the service of others"

– Mahatma Gandhi.

Born and raised in a rural town in the southeastern region of California, Sedalia Sanders imbibed the significance of community and fostered a profound zeal for altruism from an early age. Growing up as part of a nine-sibling family, tending to the needs of others became an instinct, consequently influencing Sedalia's educational path. This journey led her to attain a degree in medical technology from the College of Medical Technology an affiliate of the University of Minnesota and a bachelor's in business administration from the University of Phoenix, all rooted in her innate desire to serve.

After completing her graduation, Sedalia returned to California, armed with her medical expertise, business acumen, unwavering passion, and a resolute commitment to serving the community. These qualities paved the way for a successful career at a regional hospital. In due time, she ascended to the role of a representative of the medical community, securing a position on the Board of Trustees for the largest medical center in the region. It was during this tenure that her dedication to service drew the attention of the Mayor and City Council, resulting in her appointment to temporarily fill the position vacated by a retiring Councilmember.

The decision to run for re-election to retain the Council seat was a formidable challenge. If successful, not only would she become the Council's first black woman in over a century, but she would also make history as the city's inaugural black woman Councilwoman. Recognizing the significance of this moment for younger generations of women who might tread a similar path, Sedalia understood the weight of the choice. This profound emotional impetus compelled her to delve into her innermost reservoirs of strength, dedicating herself entirely to the cause of public service.

Throughout her campaign, Sedalia rekindled her commitment to the community, an act that garnered support from a diverse range of individuals. Drawn to her compassionate nature and inclusive viewpoints, people rallied behind her.

"I knew I could do it! Sedalia exclaimed as she reflected on that intense test of faith in herself. It was important for me to become a strong community advocate, represent everyone, and connect to people who may or may not vote for me. I was a quick study and immediately went to everyone to ask questions, actively listen, and learn."

After securing her initial election and subsequently retaining her seat, she went on to dedicate over 27 years to her role as a Councilmember, in addition to serving five times as Mayor. However, her commitment to public service didn't conclude there. Sedalia went on to become a prominent figure at both the state and national levels when she was elected as the President of the League of California Cities and appointed to the board of the

National League of Cities. Her efforts in the realm of national politics captured the attention of Governor Pete Wilson, leading to her appointment to his task force on Rural Competitiveness and other education focused initiatives. Fully devoted to these projects, Sedalia steadfastly advocated for matters of significance to rural cities

Her advice to the younger generation of women leaders is simple and yet meaningful. "As a person who was born during WWII, I've witnessed many social and economic changes as well as shifts in racial and gender beliefs. To be a successful leader, you must treat your job as if it's a matter of life or death for people. Make sure the decisions you make have the most positive impact for the people in your community. It's not about your title. People must believe in you and your ability. This approach to leadership is something I carried with me from my medical career through today, and has served me well."

It's Just What I Do

Dressed in their Sunday best and ready for additional fellowship over a meal following the local church service, the group of men hurriedly made their way into the local chicken restaurant, making no eye contact with the homeless man asking for change outside. Attempting to find odd jobs wasn't working out, so asking for any change from strangers seemed to be the only option to be able to eat. A quarter, a dime, anything would have sufficed. This day was particularly rough as it was looking like he might go hungry again. William was used to being invisible. People walk on by as if ignoring his plight will make him disappear.

The streets of Detroit can be cruel and the hungry young man knew all too well the risks at night. William wanted so badly to be self-sufficient, but tough times had fallen and today, despite his efforts to find work, was evidence that his situation wasn't improving.

"Can you spare some change, ma'am?" William's hope was dwindling.

"You're hungry? Come with me!"

Dr. Bedelia Brown, escorted the young man through the door's of Popeye's Chicken.

"He can't be in here," exclaimed the worker from behind the counter.

"He's with me," Ms. Brown proclaimed.

"Now you get yourself whatever you want." Ms. Brown instructed the young man. "I don't care if you get 3 or 30 pieces, you get whatever you want."

Irritated by a lack of compassion, Ms. Brown then turned to the group of men from church, "Didn't you listen to anything the pastor told you? You should be ashamed of yourselves."

William's eyes grew wide and he smiled at Ms. Brown. "I know you."

"No you do not," Ms. Brown proclaimed.

"Yes, I do." Insisted William.

"No! You don't know me." Ms. Brown insisted, knowing her cover was blown.

"Yes, Ms. Brown, you're the one who fed the shelter!"

"Your order is up," the Popeye's employee motioned toward Ms. Brown and William.

With bags of chicken in hand, Ms. Brown and William made their way out of the restaurant.

"Now what are you doing, way across town?" Ms. Brown scoldingly challenged William.

"I was hoping to find work. You know, small cleaning jobs and such." William shared.

"You know the streets aren't safe at night. You need a bed. You are safe at the shelter. You give me just a minute. I'm going to make sure that you have a bed tonight."

This story was shared by SOUL Foundation

(SOwing Unconditional Love Foundation) founder, Dr. Bedelia Brown and illustrates leadership in action. Did this leadership take place in a boardroom or in the confines of an office building? The answer is no. It happened in the trenches of life, while going about her day. How many times have you and I witnessed someone like William and walked on by?

Dr. Brown is on a mission to feed the hungry and help as many people in her community as possible and it's just what she does. Dr. Brown learned from an early age to never "look down your nose" toward another person. This sage wisdom was imparted by her auntie., "If you are able to help, help."

The narrative of Dr. Brown's encounter with William is a vivid embodiment of a principle that stands at the heart of this book: leadership is not about titles or positions, but about impact, influence, and inspiration. It's about seeing a need and stepping up to the plate to meet that need, regardless of whether or not it falls within your official scope of duties or expectations. Dr. Brown's action that day in the restaurant was a significant act of leadership that was both courageous and compassionate.

Examining the Elements

But let's break down the elements of her leadership and how they can serve as a template for young women seeking to lead boldly and break free from limited beliefs that might hold them back.

Boldness

Dr. Brown wasn't afraid to step out of her comfort zone and defy societal conviction. Just as Dr. Brown did, you can inspire others through your actions, influence them to be better, and make a lasting impact. Remember, leadership is not always about being in command; it is about serving others, taking action, and leading change, regardless of where you are or who you are. Like Dr. Brown, let your leadership journey be a beacon for others, illuminating the path of courage, compassion, and change.

By showcasing a range of leadership styles and strategies, we all have the ability to inspire and encourage the next generation of girls to become versatile, adaptable, and successful leaders.norms. She didn't let the judgmental eyes of others or the uncomfortable atmosphere in the restaurant stop her. This is a crucial aspect of leadership, to have the courage to do what is right, even if it means standing alone.

Empathy

It's not just about recognizing a need but also feeling the pain of the other person. Empathy is about putting yourself in their shoes, understanding their predicament, and feeling compelled to alleviate their hardship. Dr. Brown empathized with William's hunger and hardship and used it as a driving force to take action.

Action Recognizing a problem and feeling empathy is a starting point, but true leadership manifests in action. Dr. Brown didn't just feel sorry for William; she took the initiative to feed him and ensure his safety.

Influence

By inviting William to dine with her, Dr. Brown also impacted the men from the church and the worker behind the counter. Her actions sent a powerful message about compassion and kindness, perhaps stirring up their conscience.

Service

Dr. Brown's actions weren't about receiving praise or acknowledgement. She was genuinely serving another human being in need, a perfect depiction of Gandhi's quote that starts this chapter.

What makes this story powerful is not the grandeur of the stage on which it was played out but the profound effect of Dr. Brown's action. As young women seeking to lead and impact the world around you, remember that leadership isn't about the spotlight, it's about the changes you can make, no matter how small they may seem.

Moreover, understand that leadership can be manifested anywhere and anytime, and you don't need to be in a prominent position or have substantial resources to make a difference. Each one of us has the potential to be a leader, just like Dr. Brown. All it requires is courage, empathy, initiative, the will to influence, and the heart to serve.

Dr. Brown's story underscores that leadership is not a destination, but a journey of self-transformation. As young women, we are all on a path to discover our unique brand of leadership. We must be open to challenging our limited beliefs and learning from the ordinary yet extraordinary women who lead courageously and selflessly in their own unique ways, like Dr. Brown.

In the words of another great leader, Eleanor Roosevelt, "Do one thing every day that scares you." Do one thing that pushes you out of your comfort zone, one thing that brings you closer to understanding the power of your potential. Leadership, after all, is a journey of discovery, of courage, and of service. And the world needs more leaders like Dr. Brown - women who are not afraid to lead the charge for change, to uplift others, and to inspire through their actions.

After all, leadership is not about being in command, it's about being in service - to people, to causes, and to the world. So go forth, find your inner Dr. Brown, and lead with courage, compassion, and conviction. Because the world is waiting for your unique, bold, and brave leadership.

Taking Action

Strategies for Identifying and Cultivating a Unique Leadership Style

Personal Leadership Inventory

Spend a week noting moments when you naturally take charge, solve a problem, or inspire others. Analyze these instances to identify your natural leadership style.

Discover Your Empathy Quotient

Learn from Dr. Susan and practice active listening and open-ended questions to better understand the people around you.

Adopt the 'Why Not Me?' Mindset

Take a cue from Simone and ask yourself, "Why not me?" whenever you encounter a situation that needs leadership.

Be Compassionately Courageous

Inspired by Dr. Bedelia Brown, don't walk by a

problem that you can help solve. Whether it's someone in immediate need or a larger issue, step up if you can make a difference.

Cultivate Resilience through Micro-Challenges

Like many women in leadership, resilience is key. Practice this by putting yourself in uncomfortable but non-threatening situations.

Commit to Lifelong Learning

Just like Dr. Susan, don't ever think you know it all. Each month, focus on learning something new that aligns with your leadership goals.

Create Your 'Courage Journal'

Like Principal Anita, document difficult decisions and reflect on them during times of doubt.

Service-Based Leadership

Inspired by Sedalia Sanders, find a cause that you are passionate about and offer your skills to make a positive impact.

Act in the Moment

Learn from Dr. Bedelia Brown's spontaneous yet impactful action. Sometimes leadership requires quick, compassionate decisions without awaiting recognition or approval.

Key Takeaways

- **Diversity in Leadership:** Different situations require different types of leadership. Each woman in this chapter demonstrates that leadership styles can and should vary.

- **Leadership Beyond Titles:** Leadership is not confined to boardrooms or official roles. As Dr. Bedelia Brown shows, true leadership happens in the trenches of daily life.

- **The Power of Empathy:** Empathy, as shown by Dr. Susan and Dr. Bedelia Brown, is a critical component in impactful leadership.

- **Resilience and Grit:** No matter the adversity, the ability to push through and make courageous decisions defines a strong leader.

- **Influence over Authority:** As seen with Simone, sometimes you don't need a title to make a significant impact.

- **Service as Leadership:** Both Sedalia Sanders and Dr. Bedelia Brown demonstrate that serving others is a potent form of leadership.

- **Spontaneity in Leadership:** Leadership isn't always planned. Dr. Bedelia Brown's story exemplifies that sometimes the most impactful acts are those done in the spur of the moment.

CHAPTER 7

CREATING AN INCLUSIVE AND DIVERSE WORK ENVIRONMENT

"Never doubt the power of a woman's intuition, for it is the compass that guides her to greatness."

– Eleanor Roosevelt

When we think of leadership, we often envision a solitary figure, standing tall and alone at the helm. But true leadership is not about standing apart; it's about creating spaces where everyone feels seen, heard, and valued. It's about leading the charge for inclusivity and diversity, smashing through the barriers of limited beliefs and creating environments where every individual, regardless of gender, race, religion, or background, can thrive.

Creating an inclusive and diverse work environment is not just a noble goal; it is a critical requirement for fostering the next generation of dynamic and effective female leaders. It is about cultivating a culture that thrives on innovation, encourages everyone to unlock their potential, and celebrates differences instead of being threatened by them.

This chapter delves into the pivotal strategies for addressing unconscious biases and fostering diversity, equity, and inclusion. We will traverse the terrain of implementing policies and practices that support all team members, creating a workplace that is not merely tolerant but truly welcoming and supportive.

Embracing Diversity as Human-Centered Leadership in Conservation at WWF

Cultivating an inclusive and diverse workplace is not merely an altruistic endeavor but a strategic one. This principle is illustrated through the work of Britta Justesen, the Regional Director of the World Wildlife Fund (WWF). It's important to delve into how her views and experiences resonate with the core values of diversity and inclusion, and the profound impact they have on both the WWF and society at large.

Studies have shown that diversity and inclusion can drive innovation, increase productivity, and positively impact business performance (McKinsey, 2015). From the individual to the collective, the benefits are clear. For WWF, embracing diversity and inclusion is more than a moral imperative; it's an operational necessity. This focus has facilitated creative problem-solving in conservation efforts and outreach strategies, making the organization more adaptable and resilient.

Justesen observes that we're at a strange crossroads. "We are in a weird corner. Older males seem threatened by women like they are losing something. We've made great strides, but it's going to take some systemic changes to get people on the same playing field. We play like we have it, but it's made of matchsticks. We've got a lot more work to do."

Her insights into the need for systemic change and the challenges of creating an inclusive environment are starkly honest. She's been at the forefront of shifting WWF's culture, ensuring that everyone around the table feels valued and seen, fostering a sense of belonging that transcends mere tokenism.

WWF is an organization that transcends borders and cultures, working to conserve endangered species and ecosystems worldwide. To achieve this, they rely on a network of scientists, activists, local communities, and governments, all of which encompass diverse backgrounds and perspectives. Justesen's leadership in promoting diversity within WWF is not a superficial act of virtue but a pragmatic strategy. The organization benefits from a variety of perspectives, ideas, and methodologies that stem from different cultural, gender, and socioeconomic backgrounds. It enables WWF to approach conservation with greater empathy and creativity.

When considering the role of younger generations, particularly Millennials and Generation Z, Justesen finds that they are more than just casual observers; they have a profound understanding of a critical cultural shift. These generations are marked by an intrinsic need for greater connection, inclusiveness, and purpose-driven work. The change they demand aligns with social justice, climate change, and equality, reflecting their desire to see themselves as part of a broader, interconnected world community. WWF recognizes this demand and has tailored its approach to youth engagement accordingly. They actively encourage younger generations to play meaningful roles in environmental stewardship, offering educational programs, volunteer opportunities, and platforms for youthful voices. Justesen's belief in the power of youth to drive significant change has led WWF to embrace the energy and creativity of younger generations, fostering an environment where innovation can flourish. This engagement not only supports WWF's immediate goals but plants seeds for future leadership, creating a lasting connection between youth and the environment.

As we look at the ecosystem of the business world, Justesen points out the need for female perspectives as a great equalizer. She explains that women often think more about people, not simply the bottom line, highlighting a unique perspective on leadership within WWF and beyond. This perspective is valuable in an organization like WWF, where connection, collaboration, and a holistic understanding of complex issues are essential. Women's leadership in WWF often emphasizes empathy, understanding human-nature connections, community needs, and social dynamics. This focus on people and relationships translates to a more collaborative leadership style that enables better teamwork between different stakeholders, such as scientists, local communities, governments, and other NGOs.

Justesen's leadership showcases how a woman-led approach can significantly impact conservation efforts, aligning perfectly with WWF's goals and making the organization more effective in its mission. Beyond her role, Justesen's insights into women's leadership pave the way for more women to take on leadership roles within conservation. By emphasizing the unique value women bring, she helps foster an environment where women can thrive and lead, creating a model for businesses and organizations seeking to make a positive impact on both people and the planet.

Shifting the Narrative

The shift in leadership perspective that Justesen champions transcends mere strategy; it is a paradigm change. The outdated notion that women must 'act like men' to be successful has long been a barrier to authentic leadership. Justesen's approach challenges this convention, actively fostering an environment within WWF where women can embrace their unique qualities without fear of judgment or stereotyping.

This empowerment isn't merely symbolic; it has a tangible positive impact on WWF's approach to conservation. By encouraging women to lead with their strengths, including empathy, collaboration, and a more human-centered perspective, Justesen's leadership has enriched the organization's culture.

It has allowed for a broader understanding of conservation that considers not just environmental factors but human needs and connections. This shift recognizes that conservation is not merely a scientific endeavor but a deeply human one, and it allows WWF to approach its mission with more innovation, flexibility, and inclusiveness.

A Lesson from the Animal Kingdom

Justesen provides an insightful comparison between leadership and lessons from the animal kingdom, and it is not only illustrative, but profound. Drawing from nature's wisdom, she observes that if an addition to the social structure is perceived as enriching, the female animal develops a powerful sense of belonging and kinship. This natural occurrence is more than an analogy; it's a blueprint for human interaction within WWF.

It guides the creation of an inclusive and diverse environment where all staff can express their authentic selves. This sense of belonging has a cascading effect, enhancing organizational cohesion, teamwork, and overall effectiveness. The richness of diversity becomes a strength, mirroring the natural world's complexity and adaptability. Within WWF, this comparison has shaped policies and practices that value differences, fostering an environment where everyone can thrive.

This natural wisdom has enabled WWF to approach conservation with a nuanced understanding, recognizing that environmental stewardship requires harmony, not just with nature, but within the human fabric that engages with it.

Justesen's leadership in WWF embodies the very principles of diversity, inclusion, and empathy that the world needs. It is critical that our future generations follow her lead. Her insights offer valuable lessons not just for WWF but for all organizations seeking to create a more inclusive, equitable, and dynamic workplace.

As we forge ahead, we must remember that our journey is about illuminating the path for others to follow, building on the progress made, and continuing to push for systemic change.

By embracing the lessons shared by Justesen, we can inspire the next generation of female leaders to lead the charge, create more inclusive, diverse, and equitable environments, and craft a brighter future for all.

Roots of Resilience

A Journey to the City of Trees

Wendy Aguilar's story isn't merely a tale of triumph; it's a melody that sings of resilience, ambition, and the spirit of an unstoppable woman. Born in a small village in Guatemala, Wendy's journey to success began with the unbreakable courage of her mother. A woman brave enough to, with her husband, leave her children behind with dreams of building a brighter future in the land of opportunity - the United States.

Finally at the age of 10, arriving in a new world, not speaking a word of English, could have been a barrier for many. But not for Wendy. The language wasn't an obstacle; it was a challenge, a pathway to her dream. Every word learned was a step closer to becoming the woman she wanted to be.

Wendy's parents worked tirelessly in manual labor jobs, hoping to ensure a better life for their children. They planted the seeds of opportunity, and Wendy nourished them with her relentless dedication. While waitressing, her unique charm, professionalism, and customer service caught the eye of someone in the news industry. And just like that, a Hollywood story unfolded. From journalism school to an intern position with ABC7, Los Angeles - Wendy's dreams were unfolding right before her eyes.

The story of Wendy is filled with poignant details from finding herself *inspired by* the words of Oprah, while working on assignment to being esteemed as *the inspiration.*

Not long after joining ABC7, Wendy had the unimaginable opportunity to go on assignment at a school in East Los Angeles. Not knowing who the surprise speaker was, Wendy was blown away when the mayor took the podium and introduced Oprah Winfrey. For Wendy, it was more than just a dream come true; Oprah's presence and her words struck a profound chord. Oprah spoke about her childhood dreams, memories devoid of trees and pools, and how she had yearned for six specific trees and a single pool of water her own. This simple desire was more than just an object or a number; it was a promise to herself, a goal to strive for. One morning, as Oprah sat sipping her tea, she looked out to see not just the pool she sat in front of, but the six trees surrounding.

As she looked beyond the six trees, she saw trees as far as her eyes could see, thousands of other trees that had sprung from her hard work. It was then, Oprah recalled that she realized the universe's boundless gifts.

This story of dreams, manifestation, and gratitude resonated deeply with Wendy, shaping her mindset and becoming a driving force in her life. The vision of six trees and a pool wasn't just Oprah's dream—it became a metaphor for ambition, hard work, and the unexpected blessings that follow. It was a symbol of aspiration.

Fast forward past her days as an award-winning television anchor to her current role as a communications professional for Sacramento Fire, educating and empowering, Wendy is a catalyst for change and an embodiment of manifested dreams. When Wendy was on her way to Sacramento for a job interview, seeing the sign "welcome to Sacramento City of Trees" was not just a coincidence; it was a profound affirmation of her path. The words connected her to Oprah's story, her dreams, and her journey towards realizing them. It encapsulated her hard-fought battle to master English, her passion for journalism, and the incredible opportunity she received while waitressing.

The City of Trees became a manifestation of Wendy's growth, a realization that she had made it, that her dreams were within reach. It was a reminder of her mother's courage to build a better life, her own determination, and the many unexpected opportunities that came her way. The trees were no longer just physical entities; they were symbols of Wendy's aspirations, success, and the promise of a future filled with even more possibilities.

Humbled and taken aback when referred to as a "rockstar" and an "inspiration," by an attendee at one of her many public speaking events. To Wendy, she is just "doing what she does," yet, anyone witnessing her in action just can't help but feel the truth in those words. Wendy's presence radiates determination, not just to achieve her goals but to uplift those around her.

Creating an inclusive and diverse work environment is part of Wendy's legacy. She isn't just a journalist; she's a beacon for change, demonstrating that our backgrounds don't have to define us, but they can refine us. From her mother's bravery to her own fearless pursuit of education and career, Wendy exemplifies what it means to lead the charge for change.

What's most touching about Wendy's journey is the way it resonates with the universal dream. Her story speaks to anyone who has ever felt the pull of something greater, a calling that demands courage, perseverance, and faith in oneself. Wendy's story is an inspiration, a testament to the fact that no matter where you start, your dreams are valid, reachable, and waiting for you to embrace them.

"Don't be afraid to try, and don't be afraid to fail," says Wendy.

In Wendy Aguilar, we find not just a successful journalist but a symbol of the power of perseverance, the beauty of self-belief, and the wisdom of never losing sight of what truly matters. Her story isn't just her own; it's a reflection of the power in all of us to change our future and our communities.

Embrace your dreams, reach for your stars, and never forget the path that leads you to your own City of Trees. Wendy's story is a guide, a beacon, and most importantly, a heartfelt inspiration that sings a song of possibility for all of us. Her story continues to inspire, reminding us all that dreams can come true, and that we are all capable of reaching our own "City of Trees." Let her story be a reminder that your dreams are your own City of Trees, waiting for you to claim them.

Talent Knows No Boundaries

In a world that often strives for perfection, there exist unsung heroes whose journeys inspire us to reimagine the boundaries of human potential and challenge the preconceived notions that we tightly hold. Meet Jennifer Kumiyama, a devoted disability advocate, whose courage, determination, and unyielding belief in the power of change has inspired a generation. Through the lens of her life, we are invited to witness the transformation of adversity into strength, discrimination into advocacy, and obstacles into stepping stones towards a more inclusive and compassionate society.

Jennifer was born with Arthrogryposis (AMC), a condition that occurs once in approximately one out of every 3,000 births. When her doctors proposed amputating her limbs, her mother and father vehemently refused. Through the age of eight, she underwent several major surgeries aimed at improving her mobility. Jennifer, the oldest of six children, was raised in a family that celebrated her differences, viewing them as qualities that made her unique. With unwavering support from her parents, a strong sense of faith, and love of her family, Jennifer's physical limitations never hindered her from embracing life to the fullest.

During her formative years, Jennifer was immersed in a world of music. She regularly attended church services with her father, a Catholic, and her maternal grandfather, a Baptist, exposing her to a rich tapestry of musical styles. Her stepmother, a jazz instrumentalist, shared her passion for music and instilled the love of the piano in Jennifer.

During kindergarten, Jennifer was drawn to musical theater, and it was there she discovered her lifelong passion for the performing arts. For her, music became the medium through which she could freely express herself and navigate the complex emotions of being a multiracial child with a disability. Music served as the unifying thread that connected her to her innermost feelings.

By the age of six, Jennifer had already embarked on her musical journey, starting as a choir singer at Holy Innocents Catholic Church in Long Beach, California. As she grew older, her passion for music expanded, leading her to participate in local theater groups, school choirs, and even play the drums in a community orchestra. It wasn't until college that Jennifer truly realized her calling as a professional singer and performer, prompting her to pursue a formal music education. Her educational path led her through voice studies at Riverside Community College, followed by continued pursuits at Long Beach City College and California State University, Long Beach.

The idea that society might not readily embrace a performer in a wheelchair didn't deter Jennifer from pursuing her dream of a professional career in the spotlight. Her journey began with an audition for Warner Bros reality TV show "PopStars2." To everyone's delight, Jennifer not only secured a spot, but also quickly became a sensation, earning recognition as the "girl in a wheelchair." Her newfound confidence propelled her closer to her lifelong aspiration.

In 2002, Jennifer faced an extensive audition process that led to a remarkable breakthrough. She was cast by the internationally renowned director of opera and theater, Francesca Zambello, in Disney's "Aladdin: A Musical Spectacular." This milestone made her the first wheelchair-using performer to grace any Disney Theme Park Production. On this prestigious stage, Jennifer had the opportunity to represent the disabled community to a daily audience of over 8,000 people, hailing from all corners of the world. It was here that Jennifer uncovered her true passion: using her voice to break attitudinal barriers and demonstrate to the world that talent knows no boundaries.

Jennifer's career continued to flourish, with appearances at prominent venues in Los Angeles, California, including the Stella Adler Theater, Staples Center, and the Kodak Theater. Her acting credits boast a leading role as 'Carmen' in the Sundance Film Festival hit and Academy Award nominated film "The Sessions," as well as appearances on MTV's teenage sensation, "Awkward," and "Celebrity Undercover Boss." She has also amassed numerous accolades, including the titles of Ms. Wheelchair California and 1st runner up for Ms. Wheelchair America.

Furthermore, she has been honored with the prestigious Jerry Stein independent Living Award from the Disabled Resource Center in Long Beach, California. Jennifer's journey serves as a testament to the power of determination and talent, proving that one's abilities should always take precedence over any perceived limitations.

Drawing inspiration from her grandmother and stepmother, who instilled in her the profound impact of our actions and importance of assisting others, Jennifer came to recognize her individual power to support her disability community. Her source of motivation expanded when she learned of Judy Heumann, renowned as the driving force behind the Americans with Disabilities movement, who became her role model within the disability community. Additionally, during her early career in the political sphere, her first boss illuminated the significance of having a seat at the policymaking table, where decisions directly affect communities.

With these compelling influences propelling her, Jennifer's mission centers on educating people and dispelling the misconception that disabilities only emerge with age. She fervently believes that disability can manifest at any point in a person's life. Her overarching objective for the disability community is to ensure that everyone, regardless of circumstances, can effortlessly traverse the streets, take a flight, and access housing that is universally accessible. Witnessing others live comfortably and witnessing the joy on their faces serves as a testament to the worthiness of her efforts.

Jennifer shares valuable advice for both her younger self and upcoming generations. She emphasizes the importance of granting oneself grace and forgiveness, especially when navigating the unique challenges of living with a disability. She also encourages individuals to maintain their resilience and perseverance, yet not overlook the crucial need for rest and self-care. Jennifer reminds us that we deserve the goodness life has to offer, and sometimes we simply just need to take a moment to breathe.

Empowering Leadership for Women of Color

"Each time a woman stands up for herself, she stands up for all women."

- Maya Angelou

Women of color have emerged as a powerful force in leadership, breaking through barriers and shattering glass ceilings in a myriad of fields and industries. Maya Angelou, Misty Copland, Kamala Harris, Angela Davis, Rosa Parks, and Harriet Tubman, historic journey to leadership positions has been marked by resilience, determination, and a commitment to driving positive change. Their remarkable stories and contributions to women of color in leadership roles, represent a rich background of diversity, strength, and innovation that has transformed the landscape of leadership worldwide.

Dr. Mary Lomax-Ghirarduzzi (formerly Wardell) is renowned for her extensive expertise and thought leadership in the field of diversity and inclusion. She is recognized for her successful implementation of inclusive strategies that embrace diversity and equity. Her recent book, titled *"Twice as Good,"* showcases her talent for using intimate storytelling and personal reflections as powerful tools to inspire women of color leadership. Dr. Lomax-Ghirarduzzi encourages them to harness their personal narratives to support others in preparing for their professional journeys. Her work challenges conventional notions of workplace identities that prioritize conformity over the unique contributions and ingenuity that women of color bring to the table.

Dr. Lomax-Ghirarduzzi's deep commitment extends to fostering inclusive organizational cultures and advocating for the well-being of women of color within these spaces. She recognizes that these environments, marked by social and cultural structures, can either propel or hinder their leadership journeys.

Leadership for women of color is a crucial and empowering concept that acknowledges the unique challenges and opportunities faced by women with racially diverse backgrounds. They often experience intersectional discrimination, where gender and race intersect to create distinct barriers and biases. Further, leadership for women of color is not only about breaking barriers, but also about creating pathways for future generations. To be effective, consider these leadership strategies and principles:

Self-Awareness

Understanding one's own identity, strengths, weaknesses, and cultural background is essential. Self-awareness helps to navigate challenges, leverage your unique perspectives and build confidence.

Resilience

Resilience is critical for any leader; however, it is especially important for women of color who may face additional obstacles. Building resilience will enable you to persevere through adversity and setbacks.

Advocacy and Allyship

Advocate for yourself and others. Encourage allies to support diversity and inclusion initiatives and speak out against bias and discrimination when you see it.

Work for more systematic change within your organizations to address inequities to create a more inclusive environment.

Embrace Intersectionality

Recognize that your identity is multifaceted, and your experiences are shaped by the intersection of race, gender, and other factors. You can embrace and celebrate this diversity in your leadership style.

Mentor and Inspire Others

As you progress in your leadership journey, mentor other women of color. Share your experiences and knowledge to inspire and help them overcome challenges.

Authentic Leadership

Remember to be true to yourself and your values. Authentic leadership for women of color is about staying genuine, and consistent in your actions and decisions.

Taking Action

Supporting Diversity, Equity and Inclusion

Self-Education

Take the initiative to educate yourself about different forms of biases—gender, racial, age-related, disabilities, and others.

Use online resources, books, or even workshops to expand your understanding.

Reflect and Question: Regularly reflect on your own assumptions and prejudices. Keep a journal to track moments when you felt that a decision or thought was influenced by bias.

Promoting Diversity, Equity, and Inclusion

Get Involved: Participate in diversity and inclusion initiatives that are available to you—whether it's a school club, a workplace resource group, or a community organization.

Cultivate a Diverse Network: Make an active effort to know people from diverse backgrounds and perspectives. This could be as simple as joining different clubs, attending diverse gatherings, or connecting online with people you wouldn't typically interact with.

Implementing Inclusive Policies and Practices

Advocate for Flexibility: If you have the opportunity to influence policies within any organizations you're part of, advocate for flexible work arrangements and a focus on work-life balance.

Be the Change: Take the initiative to address conflicts and discrimination issues that you notice.

Develop a script or talking points to address uncomfortable situations confidently.

Encouraging Open Communication

Speak Up: Whether it's a classroom, an online forum, or a community meeting, make your voice heard. Share your opinions and insights constructively.

Seek Feedback: Don't hesitate to ask for constructive feedback from mentors, peers, or even family members. Use it as a tool for growth and improvement.

Providing a Safe and Supportive Environment

Evaluate Your Spaces: Actively assess the inclusivity of environments you frequent. If you find any issues, consider taking them up with the relevant authorities.

Promote Inclusivity: Wherever you are—school, work, or social circles—initiate or participate in activities that encourage inclusivity and a sense of belonging for everyone.

Key Takeaways

- **Inclusivity is Operational:** Just like at WWF, creating an inclusive environment is not just morally right but operationally essential.

- **Systemic Changes are Necessary:** True inclusivity requires systemic changes, not just isolated efforts, as pointed out by Britta Justesen.

- **Diversity Drives Innovation:** As supported by studies and exemplified in WWF, diversity can be a catalyst for creativity and problem-solving.

- **The Power of Youth:** Millennial and Generation Z's intrinsic understanding of diversity and inclusion can be a game-changer for an organization.

- **Women's Unique Leadership Attributes:** As Justesen's leadership at WWF shows, women bring a unique, people-focused perspective that can significantly benefit organizations.

- **Resilience and Opportunity:** Wendy Aguilar's journey epitomizes how resilience can turn challenges into opportunities, emphasizing that your background can refine, not define you. Jennifer Kumiyama's experiences demonstrate the power of determination and talent, proving that one's abilities should always take precedence over any perceived limitations.

- **The Significance of Symbolism:** Wendy's City of Trees moment shows the importance of having symbols or milestones that represent your values and journey towards inclusivity.

- **Intersectionality in Leadership:** Both Justesen and Wendy show that effective leadership considers multiple facets of diversity, including gender, culture, and socio-economic background.

- **Harness Natural Wisdom:** Justesen's comparison to the animal kingdom serves as a reminder that nature itself values diversity and that we can learn valuable lessons from it.

- **A Journey, Not a Destination:** Building an inclusive and diverse environment is a continuous process, requiring constant effort and evolution.

CHAPTER 8

NURTURING FUTURE FEMALE LEADERS

"The most powerful weapon a woman can wield is her unwavering belief in her own potential."

– Marie Curie

Encouraging and supporting the next generation of female leaders is essential for continued progress towards gender equality. This chapter will focus on providing guidance, resources, and opportunities for girls and young women to pursue leadership roles. By celebrating and sharing stories of female role models, we can inspire future generations to dream big and break barriers.

Shaping Spaces, Shaping Leaders

The Blueprint for Inspiring Future Generations

Rachel McLure's story is an illuminating testament to the power of belief, resilience, and mentorship in forging a path to leadership. As a City Commissioner of Parks and Recreation and a Senior Planner for local government in Southern California, Rachel is not just an influential figure but also an inspiring mentor.

Her journey began with the support of a seasoned and sagacious female city manager who recognized Rachel's untapped potential. Encouraging her to step up to the plate, this mentor illuminated a path to leadership for Rachel. Following this invaluable support, another mentor, former director Mario Lara, genuinely invested in her professional growth, showing her the importance of empathetic leadership. It was Lara's teachings that helped Rachel understand that employees seek understanding and empathy, even when their problems cannot be immediately solved. "They just want to have someone to talk to. They want to feel that they are heard, even if you can't do anything about the situation," Rachel says.

In her life, Rachel has had role models who have personified determination and balance. Her mother, a single parent and a college professor, showed her the value of education and the art of managing life's multifaceted demands. Today, Rachel pays it forward, inspiring young women interested in architecture, embodying the same support she once received.

Rachel's insights to aspiring leaders are as profound as they are empowering: Embrace your mistakes; they are stepping stones to success. Cultivate relationships, they're your network. Exhibit kindness, it's your strength. And above all, pursue your passion relentlessly; it's the key to true fulfillment. She shares her own experience, where she learned that the pursuit of power and money can often eclipse personal happiness and family life. The wisdom she imparts from her journey encourages young women to prioritize their happiness and passion above societal expectations.

As a woman in a leadership role, Rachel acknowledges the existence of ingrained patriarchal structures, often unconscious yet inhibiting women's progress. Her hope for future workplaces is to create an environment that values outcomes over face time at the desk and encourages a fair division of family responsibilities.

Rachel firmly believes in the unique strength of women—their emotional intelligence—that can be a transformative force in decision-making, the business world, and society. She stands as a beacon of encouragement for young women, urging them to lean into this strength and use it to fuel their journey to leadership.

In sharing her story, Rachel McLure becomes a testament to the power of mentorship, resilience, and belief. She is the embodiment of inspiration for the next generation of women leaders, proving that they can redefine leadership on their terms and inspire change in the world.

Defying Predictions

A Tale of Authenticity and Resilience

High school can be the breeding ground for dreams, yet for Krystal Cardona, it was where her aspirations were bluntly dismissed. A teacher had decided her fate - she would amount to nothing more than her mother, a teenage parent confined to a small town. But Krystal was not one to accept such predictions, and this dismissal became her fuel, driving her to prove the naysayers wrong.

Today, with a Master's degree in Human Resource Management, a successful career as an educator, and authorship to her name, Krystal stands as a testament to the power of resilience and determination. She's proven her doubters wrong, and more importantly, she's proved herself right.

The definition of success is not set in stone; it's a mutable entity, shifting and transforming as one's understanding grows. For Krystal, it has morphed from ticking boxes on society's checklist to living a life molded by her values and dreams. The 9-5 grind, once her reality, is now a thing of the past. Her days are filled with cheer, swimming, soccer, baseball and a car full of laughter and youthful energy.

"Regardless of what others say about you, it's important to stay true to your core. But first, you must know what you stand for and understand yourself," Krystal emphasizes. It's a lesson she wishes she'd learned earlier, one that would have helped her fend off the pangs of imposter syndrome. If she'd known her values, her identity, she wouldn't have had to constantly strive for validation from those who didn't matter.

Krystal is an advocate for female empowerment, wanting women to grasp their potential fully, to realize the power they hold. She dreams of a society where no woman is minimized or pushed aside, where her daughter and the countless other young girls can grow up unaffected by societal biases. She believes that, in such a world, we can witness an era of unparalleled growth and transformation.

The spirit of resilience and defiance that permeates Krystal's story can be traced back to her grandparents. They swam across the border from Mexico to the U.S. twice, an illegal but desperate act, driven by the pursuit of a better life for their family. Their courage and determination are a part of Krystal's inheritance, and they form the backbone of her resolve.

Krystal sees women as superpowered beings, able to perceive the big picture, navigate through complexities with creativity, and anticipate the next steps.

Women's multifaceted roles in society, she asserts, have honed their forward-thinking abilities and broadened their perspective. This, Krystal argues, is where women add unmatched value to organizations.

In her children's book, "I Don't Know How but I Know I Will", Krystal Cardona has crafted an inspiring tale that instills the values of tenacity, self-belief, and resilience in the minds of young readers. This engaging story uses relatable characters and scenarios to express the simple but powerful message that obstacles can be overcome by perseverance and belief in oneself. Her book echoes the spirit of our guidebook, "Leading the Charge for Change: Women Inspiring Leadership," as it serves as an early catalyst to empower the future generation. Krystal aims to equip children, especially girls, with the tools they need to navigate a world full of challenges, just as our guidebook seeks to empower adult women to seize control of their narratives. Both works stress the importance of self-awareness, resilience, and the unyielding belief that one can make a significant difference. Through her writing, Krystal is paving the way for future female leaders, underscoring the importance of their voices and perspectives in shaping a better world.

In Krystal's story, we find a beacon of hope and motivation, a testament to the power of self-belief, and an impassioned plea for women's self-discovery.

The driving force that was once a negative prediction has now become a powerful narrative of resilience and defiance, a story that calls on all women to grasp their value, power, and potential.

Investment in a Life Unimagined

On a chilly evening in the heart of the Midwest, Matt Redding, owner of a financial services firm, took a detour from his usual routine. Leaving behind the world of stocks, portfolios, and clients, he volunteered at a local homeless shelter. It was there that Matt's path intersected with young Emma Martinez, a bright-eyed girl of fifteen with dreams far greater than her circumstances.

Emma, a diligent student with a penchant for numbers, lived with her struggling single mother at the shelter. Unlike most teenagers her age, Emma spent her evenings pouring over financial news, fascinated by the stock market, and dreaming of a future where she'd be a financial magnate.

Noticing Emma's financial newspaper, Matt struck up a conversation. The two talked about stocks, the future of finance, and Emma's dreams. Captivated by her intelligence and passion, Matt saw in her the potential that many might have overlooked.

"Success is where preparation and opportunity

meet," Matt fondly remembers, telling Emma. "I believe you're already prepared. Let me offer you an opportunity."

Taking her under his wing, Matt became a mentor to Emma. He provided her with internships, financial education, and a space to flourish. Emma's aptitude combined with Matt's guidance led to her rapid ascent in the financial world.

Matt often said, "True wealth isn't just in the numbers. It's in the stories we create and the lives we change." Emma became the embodiment of this mantra. Through hard work and determination, she established herself in the financial sector, and with Matt's continuous encouragement, she started her financial advisory practice.

"Every individual," Matt reflected, "has a reservoir of untapped potential. Sometimes, all they need is someone to recognize it and give it direction."

Fast forward to the present, and Emma stands tall, not just as a successful financial advisor but also as an advocate for women in finance. Her portfolio is vast, her clientele elite, and her influence undeniable.

"Matt taught me that numbers have power, but people have more," Emma reflects. "He saw potential in me when the world saw none. Today, I stand as a testament to the power of mentorship, belief, and dreams."

She is now leading the charge in mentoring young women in finance, ensuring that the cycle of empowerment continues. In her thriving practice, she often employs underprivileged young women, offering them the guidance and platform she once received from Matt.

Emma's story is a reminder that the right mentorship can propel us into futures we could only dream of. Her journey, guided by Matt's unwavering belief in her potential, showcases the incredible impact of a single act of kindness and faith.

In a world where female leadership often goes unrecognized, stories like Emma's are a beacon. They demonstrate that with the right support, women can break barriers, redefine industries, and inspire generations. Matt's insight is profound, "In every person, especially in women, lies an immense potential waiting to be harnessed. It's our duty to recognize it, nurture it, and watch it flourish."

In Emma's success story, we discover the immense transformative power of mentorship and belief. The trajectory of her life, which took a turn on that fateful evening in the homeless shelter, reiterates that no matter our background, with the right opportunities and support, we can rise, inspire, and lead.

Making a Difference, One Small Step at a Time

Cindy Seevers is an embodiment of the proverb, "It's not about how much you do, but how much love you put into what you do that counts." A mother of four spirited children, Cindy's life has always revolved around nurturing, teaching, and giving. Her belief is straightforward yet powerful, "You don't need a fancy education or money to make a difference."

Though Cindy didn't have the privilege of a high-level education or a lucrative career, she understood that the real power of change lies in consistent efforts and genuine care. When her children began attending their local school in their small Midwestern town, Cindy saw an opportunity.

Volunteering at her children's school wasn't about gaining recognition or status. It was about creating an environment where every child, regardless of their background, felt seen, heard, and empowered. Cindy often helped with organizing events, aiding teachers in classrooms, or merely sitting with a child who needed someone to talk to.

The school's library became Cindy's primary focus. It was outdated and lacked diversity in its collection. Recognizing the influence of stories on young minds, she initiated a community-wide drive to donate books. These books celebrated female heroes, diverse cultures, and powerful narratives of resilience and leadership.

Her initiative not only replenished the library with essential resources but also introduced the children to worlds, cultures, and female leaders they'd never known. Cindy often read these stories during library hours, emphasizing the values of perseverance, compassion, and leadership.

"Every story, every lesson, every act of kindness plants a seed," Cindy would say. "We might not see the tree today, but someday it will shade the future, and that's what counts."

Soon, Cindy's passion became contagious. Other parents began volunteering, contributing their skills and resources to nurture the students. Some provided tutoring, others offered life skill lessons, while some just shared their personal stories of success, failure, and resilience.

Cindy fondly recalls a young girl, Lucy. "When she looked at me, I just saw something. She had such aspiration in her eyes everytime I read to the kids books about people reaching for their dreams." She vividly remembers how inspired Lucy became by a story Cindy had read to the group about a female astronaut. Before returning to class, Lucy whispered to Cindy, "I want to be like her, but I don't know if someone like me can."

Cindy said that she felt such a pain in her heart at the statement. She knelt beside Lucy, and explained that making a difference or achieving your dreams isn't about where you come from, how much money you have, or how fancy your education is. It's about belief, hard work, and the choices you make. "I told her, you can be whoever you want to be. Remember, every leader, every astronaut, every change-maker was once a child with a dream, just like you."

As years passed, Cindy's efforts began bearing fruits in unexpected ways. Students from the school, inspired by her commitment and the environment she helped foster, went on to occupy positions of leadership, activism, and influence. Many of them became champions for female leadership and empowerment, attributing their passion to those formative years where they learned the value of compassion, resilience, and dreams.

Cindy's story underscores the immense power of community, belief, and consistent effort. Without a title, without significant resources, and without formal recognition, she managed to inspire a generation of future leaders.

Her story resonates with a vital message: Making a difference doesn't always require grand gestures. Sometimes, it's the small acts, done with great love, that leave the most profound impact. Cindy Seevers, in her gentle, unassuming way, became a beacon for future female leaders, proving that real change begins at the grassroots, in the hearts and the minds of the young.

Working to Reach Political Parity

Since the inception of women's participation in the United States government and politics, particularly during the suffrage movement, women have encountered resistance within the predominantly male-led political system. Although women have exerted substantial influence within the U.S. political arena, they are often confined to supportive roles across various government tiers. Over the past century, female political leaders in the U.S. have progressively gained prominence in policymaking, challenging enduring stereotypes. As of early 2023, women constitute approximately 51 percent of the U.S. population. However, their representation in elected positions within state legislatures stands at a modest 33 percent nationwide. While this marks the highest level of female representation in U.S. history, it underscores the ongoing effort required to achieve gender parity alongside our male counterparts in elected leadership roles.

Mary Hughes started on her journey into the political arena with a seemingly innocuous start. Following her graduation from the University of Virginia's law school, she soon discovered that practicing law didn't ignite her passion. It was during this time that a college classmate, who was working on a U.S. Senate campaign in Rhode Island, reached out to Mary, inquiring if she might be interested in contributing to the campaign effort. To her delight, Mary found herself deeply enamored with every aspect of the political process, setting the stage for her burgeoning career in politics.

Her involvement expanded as she assumed more significant roles, including a pivotal position on a Presidential campaign. These experiences solidified her conviction and passion for this line of work. Subsequently, Mary relocated to California, where she secured a position with a renowned consulting firm, affording her the opportunity to delve deeper into the intricacies of the political landscape. Her journey continued to evolve, culminating in her role as Executive Director for the California Democratic Party, next as a campaign manager for a Congressional campaign and finally with establishing her own strategic communications and political consulting firm.

As she solidified her role as a prominent campaign strategist, Mary became actively engaged with the Center for American Women and Politics (CAWP) at Rutgers University. It was through her collaboration with CAWP that Mary delved into an exploration of the root causes behind the fluctuating numbers of women in politics. She observed a recurring pattern where women would achieve significant milestones in some elections, only to encounter plateaus in subsequent ones.

Devoting substantial time and energy to analyze the data compiled by CAWP, Mary diligently sought clues to decipher the sporadic and uneven progress of women in the political sphere. After months of meticulous data scrutiny, Mary discerned recurring themes among female candidates. These commonalities include their recruitment for elected positions, the need for assistance in overcoming the typical obstacles faced by newcomers to the political arena, and guidance on the essential tools and strategies required for a successful candidacy.

Mary shared her findings with her colleagues at CAWP, giving birth to the 2012 Project. The project's primary objective was to identify and provide support to women who had not previously participated in political activities, encouraging them to run for office at various levels of government. The overarching aim was to enhance female representation in both state and federal political arenas.

Following the conclusion of the 2012 election cycle, Mary found encouragement in the nationwide project's results and shifted her focus toward refining the process. In 2013, Mary, alongside a group of founding members, introduced Close the Gap CA (CTGCA). Inspired by insights gained from the 2012 Project, CTGCA set out to recruit accomplished progressive women in strategically targeted districts with open seats, preparing them for competitive campaigns. The ultimate objective is to narrow the gender gap in the California Legislature, with the ambitious goal of achieving this by 2028.

Mary imparts valuable advice to the younger generation of women leaders. It's well-established that the presence of women in decision making positions leads to discernible shifts in policy priorities and outcomes, particularly benefiting traditionally underserved communities. Moreover, state legislatures are poised to remain key arenas for policy action and progress in the foreseeable future. Striving for gender parity ensures that women's voices are adequately and equitably represented, guaranteeing that their perspectives have the rightful influence they deserve.

What You Can Do:

Find or Be a Mentor

Take Rachel McLure's story as a blueprint. Seek mentorship or offer to mentor someone younger than you. The chain of guidance can make a substantial impact.

Resilient Mindset

Just like Krystal defied societal expectations and labels, remind yourself daily of your inner strength and capability. Turn negative predictions or setbacks into fuel for success.

Self-Audit for Core Values

Follow Krystal's advice to know your values and identity. Spend an hour making a list of your core beliefs and values. Revisit it whenever you face challenges or self-doubt.

Invest in Financial Literacy

Use Emma's story as a launchpad to delve into financial literacy. Start reading financial news, attend a seminar, or take an online course. This could be a path to both empowerment and financial independence.

Community Volunteering

In the spirit of Cindy Seevers or Mary Hughes, look for small ways to make a significant impact within your community. It could be volunteering at a library, on a political campaign, or initiating a social project that fills a gap in your local area.

Write or Share Empowering Stories

Just like Krystal and Cindy did through their books and actions, find a way to instill values of tenacity, self-belief, and resilience in the younger generation. This could be through storytelling, blogging, or even casual conversations.

Hone Your Emotional Intelligence

Embrace Rachel's insight about the unique strength of women in emotional intelligence. Consider reading books or taking courses to better understand how you can utilize emotional intelligence in leadership roles.

Initiate a Book Drive

Inspired by Cindy's actions, you could organize a book drive in your community or workplace. Focus on titles that promote diversity, empowerment, and leadership, and donate them to schools, libraries, or shelters.

Key Takeaways

- **The Power of Mentorship:** Mentorship can be the key to unlocking untapped potential. Whether it's a seasoned city manager, a financial services owner, or a community volunteer, a mentor can change the course of one's life.

- **Resilience as a Driving Force:** The stories of Krystal and Emma demonstrate that resilience can lead to unthinkable heights of success, shattering societal limitations and personal self-doubt.

- **Community Impact:** Small steps can lead to significant change. Cindy Seevers showed us that you don't need high qualifications or abundant resources to make a lasting impact in your community.

- **Emotional Intelligence and Empathy:** These soft skills are not to be underestimated. Rachel McLure and Mario Lara illustrated how crucial these traits are in leadership roles.

- **Diverse Definitions of Success:** Success is not one-size-fits-all. It can mean different things to different people at various stages in their life, be it professional growth, financial security, or community impact.

- **Know Your Values:** Understanding yourself is the first step in authentic leadership. When you know what you stand for, the external voices become less deafening, and you gain clarity in your actions.

- **Women as Multipliers:** The stories showcase how women not only excel in their fields but also act as multipliers by inspiring and opening doors for others.

- **Financial Literacy:** Understanding finances can serve as a powerful tool for independence and empowerment, as Emma's story demonstrates.

Chapter 9

Women in Historical Male-Dominated Fields

"A woman with vision empowers an entire generation to dream bigger, reach higher, and conquer the unconquerable."

– Maya Angelou

Breaking Barriers in STEM, Education and Leadership Roles

Our journey towards a more equitable world is not only about shattering glass ceilings in corporate boardrooms or gaining seats in political offices. It's also about transforming the silent corridors of academia, the crucible of knowledge and innovation, especially in the realms of Science, Technology, Engineering, and Mathematics (STEM), and leadership roles.

"Knowledge is power. But when that knowledge is shared, it becomes a beacon of inspiration that enlightens entire generations."

In the heartland of America, Angela took up the challenge of instilling a passion for STEM education in her small community. Born and raised in a small town where opportunities seemed scarce, Angela had always been fascinated by the stars above. Her fascination led her to become the first person in her town to earn a PhD in astrophysics. Today, Angela, with her keen understanding of the universe, serves as a university professor inspiring a new generation of girls to reach for the stars.

Then, halfway across the globe in a bustling Nigerian metropolis, there's Chiagozi, a charismatic leader who serves as a role model to young women. Chiagozi grew up amidst the hardships of poverty, yet she was resolute about changing her narrative. Today, she's a symbol of resilient leadership, proving to young girls in her community that their background does not define their future.

Angela and Chiagozi, though from starkly different backgrounds, share a common vision: to empower young girls through education, specifically in the traditionally male-dominated fields of STEM, and to foster female leadership in academia and boardrooms. They are testament to the resilience of women who are paving the way for future generations of female leaders, creating ripples of change that are making academia a more inclusive, diverse space.

This chapter will delve into their stories, along with insights from other remarkable women in academia. We will uncover the challenges they faced, the victories they savored, and the lessons they learned. More importantly, we will highlight how their contributions are shaping a more balanced academic and corporate landscape - one that celebrates diversity and encourages participation from all genders, including in STEM fields and leadership roles.

As we celebrate these women, we also acknowledge that there is still a long road ahead. Let their stories not just be tales of inspiration but also a clarion call to persistently pursue progress, because every step taken is a step closer to a world where no girl has to fight for her right to learn, lead, and leave a legacy. Let's embark on this enlightening journey together.

Igniting Stars on Earth

Underneath the vast expanse of the Midwestern skies, a small town lay cocooned away from the hustle and bustle of urban life. In this serene setting, the townspeople led simple lives, limited by the opportunities the town had to offer. Yet, for young Angela, the night skies painted a different picture—a vast canvas of twinkling possibilities and cosmic dreams.

Growing up, Angela's favorite moments were spent lying on her backyard grass, eyes fixed upon the stars. While others saw a beautiful night sky, she saw equations, mysteries, and the intricate dance of celestial bodies.

Her thirst for understanding these cosmic tales grew with every passing year, becoming the driving force behind her academic pursuits.

Despite the town's limited resources and prevailing notions about appropriate careers for women, Angela relentlessly chased her passion. Many nights, her only companions were the constellations above and the books she borrowed from the town's little library. Her dedication paid off when she became the first person from her town to attend a prestigious university and later earn a PhD in astrophysics.

Returning home with her doctorate, Angela took up a role that was much bigger than herself. Instead of moving to a city with ample opportunities, she chose to stay and ignite a spark for STEM in the hearts of the young boys and girls in her hometown. Recognizing the lack of resources and mentors in her early years, she was determined to ensure that the next generation would not face the same challenges.

Angela initiated after-school STEM programs, where students could tinker, experiment, and explore the vast realms of science, technology, engineering, and mathematics. Her astrophysics background added a unique flavor to these sessions. She transformed complex cosmic concepts into engaging, easy-to-understand stories and activities. Under her guidance, the school's backyard became a mini observatory, with telescopes and stargazing nights, where students could connect their learnings to the real universe above.

As the years rolled on, Angela's influence reached beyond her small community. She became a university professor, not in a bustling city's renowned institution, but in a college closer to home. Angela's teaching style was a blend of rigorous academia and heartfelt mentorship. She recognized the immense potential in young girls who reminded her of her younger self, always curious, always reaching for more.

To them, she would often say, "The universe is vast and limitless, and so is your potential. Never let boundaries, whether they're of gender, resources, or societal expectations, limit your orbit. Reach for the stars, for you are made of the very same elements they are."

Angela's journey serves as an emblem of hope and perseverance for many young women navigating the challenging terrains of STEM fields, especially in regions where such aspirations seem distant. Her story underscores the importance of representation, mentorship, and the sheer power of dreams.

In the chronicles of women breaking barriers in traditionally male-dominated fields, Angela shines bright.

Not just as an astrophysicist who unraveled the secrets of the cosmos, but as a beacon who illuminated paths for countless young minds, urging them to dream big, aim high, and traverse the universe of possibilities.

From Nigeria's Heart to Texas Dreams

Nestled in the vast landscapes of Nigeria, in a bustling metropolis teeming with life and rich culture, young Chiagozi charted her path. The chorus of hawkers, the rhythm of everyday hustle, and the melodies of traditional songs were her daily backdrop. But amidst this, the challenges of growing up in a low-income family often tried to overshadow her dreams.

Yet, for Chiagozi, these challenges were not insurmountable barriers, but catalysts driving her forward. She believed that every adversity held within it the seeds of opportunity. With tenacity and an unwavering spirit, she sought education as her beacon of hope, diving deep into books and seeking mentors who could guide her aspirations.

This quest for knowledge led her to discover her passion for STEM. While these fields were often seen as the domain of men, Chiagozi's brilliance and determination shone through, proving that talent and ambition knew no gender.

Her journey was not without its fair share of naysayers. Many questioned her audacity to dream beyond traditional roles. Yet, every critique only solidified her resolve. She often recalled the wisdom of her grandmother, who'd say, "Your roots give you strength, but it's your wings that determine how high you soar."

Soar she did. Her resilience and accomplishments eventually paved the way for a scholarship, and Chiagozi found herself transitioning from the familiar streets of Nigeria to the expansive horizons of Texas.

In Texas, she became not just a student but a beacon for many. Her leadership and charisma made her a role model, especially for young immigrant girls trying to find their footing in a new land. She initiated STEM programs tailored for these young minds, ensuring they had the guidance she once yearned for.

Chiagozi's story reverberated with a powerful message: where you come from does not dictate where you can go. She became a living testament to the power of dreams, perseverance, and the importance of uplifting those who follow in your footsteps. Her story proves that when women take charge of their destiny, they not only achieve greatness but also pave the way for others to do the same.

Vibrant Resilience

In the rich and fertile farmlands of Northern California, the story of Sandra unfolds—a tale that weaves together resilience, family legacy, and an unyielding pursuit of excellence. A third-generation Japanese-American, Sandra's heritage is an intricate tapestry, woven with strands of perseverance and triumph.

Her grandmothers, brave and adventurous mail-order brides from Japan, crossed oceans to embrace destinies unknown in the States. They carried dreams within their hearts, dreams that would be nurtured and handed down through generations. Sandra's parents' romance was an extraordinary testament to human strength. Their love story blossomed in the confined and somber world of internment camps, a profound connection that transcended barriers and symbolized hope amidst despair.

The family's farming life was etched with hardship, yet it was a crucible where Sandra's character was forged. The land her grandparents toiled, although not theirs to own because of laws that prevented it due their Japanese immigrant heritage, was a stage where Sandra learned the virtues of diligence, self-reliance, and determination. These lessons were not simply learned but lived, shaping her very soul.

Her older brother's journey mirrors Sandra's own resilience. Facing challenges with language misconceptions from others due to being raised speaking only Japanese, he refused to be confined by others' judgments. He led the California Coastal Commission, Tahoe Conservancy, and the Sierra Nevada Conservancy. His recognition from several governors, legislators, and resource agency directors and the Lake Tahoe community became a beacon, a reminder of what determination could achieve. He stood as a symbol of her family's indomitable spirit.

Sandra's educational odyssey was filled with mentors who opened doors to intellectual wonderment. Dr. Emmy Werner, both a guide and friend, inspired Sandra with her humor and academic brilliance. At Stanford, Dr Robert Hess professor showed Sandra how academics could be productive, collaborative, and joyful, how boundaries could be transcended with enthusiasm and love. Her cohorts at Stanford became a beautiful example of support and friendship. University life broadened her horizons both personally and professionally.

Her caring nature manifested through teaching Sunday school during her youth, tutoring underprivileged children before she was old enough to drive and guiding an overlooked high school graduate on Kauai who toward a hopeful future in college on Kauai. These acts of kindness were not mere gestures but reflections of Sandra's innate need to uplift others.

Sandra's professional life blossomed, marked by triumphs and deep satisfaction. Leading research teams, she led a positive shift in women's collaboration in academia. Her insights are not just observations but profound understandings of a world moving toward unity and shared success.

"If I had a magic wand," Sandra muses, "Freedom is having no fear." Her wish is for women to be free from fear, abuse, and harm, and to be themselves unapologetically. Her words of wisdom resonate with courage: "Don't be afraid to take risks... There's no shame... Failure is okay; you aren't going to crumble."

Family remains Sandra's anchor, each member contributing to the person she became. Her story is not merely her own but a collective narrative of those who shaped, loved and stood by her. From her mother's practicality and father's curiosity to her husband's unwavering encouragement. Her sister Connie, two sons, and mother-in-law's unconditional love all contribute to the strong academic force and nurturing woman she has become.

Sandra's story is a vibrant symphony of human experience. It resonates with a universal truth about resilience, compassion, mentorship, and the transcendent power of love. Her journey, from humble beginnings to influential academia, stands as an inspiring testament to what one can achieve with heart, passion, and unrelenting grace.

Knocking Down Barriers to Build Future Generations

By her own account, Robin Thorne was a late bloomer when it came to her higher educational journey. She started college eight years after high school, all while being a single mother and managing other challenging circumstances that ultimately categorized her as a non-traditional student. However, Robin was resolute in her determination not to have any regrets about not trying. There were two things she remained certain of: her unwavering commitment to improving the lives of both her and her son, and her unequivocal aspiration to become an engineer.

Robin was on public assistance and participated in the work study program during college while pursuing a major in Engineering at the Community College of Philadelphia. She went on to earn a Chemical Engineering degree from Drexel University College of Engineering. Throughout her time at Drexel, driven by a steadfast resolve to dispel misconceptions about women in construction and STEM fields, Robin began inviting her professional colleagues to accompany her during readings at her son's kindergarten class.

In due course, she expanded this outreach by conducting engaging science experiments with the students. It soon became evident to Robin that, for many of these young learners, it was their first encounter with a woman of color actively involved in the world of science, a male nurse, or a black executive.

Following her graduation from Drexel, Robin embarked on her chemical engineering career in Pennsylvania. Soon after, she took a courageous leap of faith when she was offered a position as a foam manufacturing engineer and relocated with her son to California to pursue opportunities in the environmental, health, and safety sectors. In 2009, Robin laid the foundation for CTI Environmental, Inc., an engineering and specialized construction firm, which has since grown into a leading organization within the industry.

In 2018, a pivotal moment arose when Robin's firm was entrusted with the significant task of demolishing a federal prison. As she meticulously prepared for the project, she began to recognize substantial educational potential within the realm of demolition for individuals interested in this career. Fueled by her enthusiasm for these opportunities, she made a steadfast commitment to increasing awareness about demolition as a viable career path that could lead to a respectable income. To initiate this educational outreach to the community, she launched a demolition program, subsequently expanding into STEM programs, as she realized the diverse array of career possibilities within this field.

According to data from the National Association of Women in Construction, women constituted 10.9 percent of the total U.S. workforce in 2022. Moreover, in the United States, women typically earn an average of 82.9 percent of what men make across all professions. Notably, the gender pay gap is narrower within the construction sector, where women earn an average of 95.5 percent of their male counterparts' earnings.

With her dedication to empowering women to realize their potential in any chosen endeavor, Robin recognized her ability to support college students navigating non-traditional paths. These students may not necessarily find themselves on the Dean's list or face unique challenges, but they have ambitions of pursuing careers in STEM fields. Drawing from her own life journey, Robin understood that the key isn't the timing of one's start, but the unwavering commitment to persevere and achieve. This realization became the driving force behind DemoChicks.

In 2019, Robin established DemoChicks as a non-profit organization with a profound mission: to act as a catalyst and multiplier, igniting the potential of young girls by revealing and sharing unconventional routes to careers in architecture, construction, and engineering. The overarching goal is to enhance their future prospects and provide them with valuable mentorship and guidance on excelling in their chosen non-traditional fields. In essence, DemoChicks knocks down barriers to build up future generations.

Robin was driven by the desire to ensure that young women in historically underserved communities were aware of others who looked like them and were actively pursuing STEM careers. She fondly remembers that it wasn't until her participation in a summer research program at Spelman College that she had the opportunity to meet numerous other black women with advanced degrees. While she had admired the work of a black faculty member at her community college, she was the sole individual she knew with such a high level of academic achievement. During her time at Spelman, Dr. Sylvia Bozeman, who led the math department, emerged as a powerful role model for Robin.

Today, DemoChicks stands as an integral part of the community, having welcomed close to 300 young women and girls into its program. This includes their active engagement in a mentoring program, industry day events, and thought-provoking panel discussions. Furthermore, the organization has had the privilege of granting multiple $2500 scholarships to Long Beach college women pursuing STEM degrees.

Robin's advice for aspiring young leaders: first and foremost, know what motivates you, and understand who you are, so you can be true to yourself. Continuously strive for self-improvement, driven by your own desire for growth. Prioritize networking as it is important to master the art of building meaningful connections with others and genuinely caring about their journeys. Find a mentor, someone who can tell you in 15 minutes what it took them 15 years to learn. And finally, don't be afraid to dream or limit yourself to your current circumstances—remember you have the power to achieve and become anything you choose.

What You Can Do:

Find Your Starry Night

Whether it's gazing at stars like Angela or navigating urban landscapes like Chiagozi, recognize the inspiration that surrounds you. Use that inspiration to fuel your academic and professional aspirations.

Connect with Like-minded Mentors

Seek out individuals who share your passion, whether they are teachers, community leaders, or online forums dedicated to your field of interest. Their advice could be the turning point in your journey. Like Robin, find someone who can help you realize your goal.

Create Your Own Opportunities

If your community lacks the resources you need, consider how you can fill that gap. Perhaps you can start a small weekend club dedicated to STEM or leadership skills, just like Angela, Chiagoz, and Robin initiated educational programs.

Break Your Own Glass Ceiling

Sometimes the barrier is not societal but internal. Aim to surpass your own expectations, not just those set by others. This could be anything from submitting an application to a top-tier university to leading a community project.

Tell Your Story

Consider sharing your own challenges and victories through blogs, local community talks, or social media. Your story could serve as inspiration for others, much like Sandra's family story serves as her anchor.

Lean Into Your Roots

Just as Chiagozi drew strength from her culture and Sandra from her family history, and Robin from her non-traditional educational journey, you too can find strength in your own roots. Your background, however challenging, can be a source of immense power.

Be a Beacon

Once you've paved your own way, don't forget to light the path for others. Mentorship isn't always formal; sometimes, it's about providing guidance and encouragement to those who are a few steps behind you.

Fight Your Own Battle But Not Alone

While it's your own struggle to qualify and excel in male-dominated fields, the support system from your friends, family, and mentors can be invaluable.

Remain Resilient

On your path, you will face setbacks just like Sandra's family and Angela did, but the resilience to continue is what sets you apart. Learn from each experience and keep pushing forward.

Key Takeaways

- **Representation Matters:** Angela, Chiagozi, and Robin highlighted the power of being a visible woman in male-dominated fields. Their presence alone serves as inspiration for other young girls to aspire more.

- **Resilience Is Non-Negotiable:** Whether it's overcoming societal stereotypes, as in Chiagozi's case, or the limitations of a small town, like Angela, resilience is often the cornerstone of success.

- **The Impact of Mentorship:** Every individual in the chapter, from Sandra, Angela, or Robin either had a mentor or became one. The cycle of mentorship is crucial for growth and paving the way for others.

- **Roots as Strength:** Chiagozi's Nigerian background, Angela's small-town upbringing, and Sandra's family history serve not as limitations but as foundations upon which they built their dreams.

- **Inclusivity and Diversity:** The stories underline the necessity of creating more inclusive environments, both in academia and in leadership roles. They serve as proof that diversifying these fields leads to richer, more effective outcomes.

- **Empowerment Through Education:** Across different continents and backgrounds, education emerges as a powerful tool for empowerment, opening doors and shattering glass ceilings.

- **The Strength of Community:** The examples of these women show that individual success has community-wide effects. By uplifting themselves, they uplift those around them, triggering a virtuous cycle of growth and empowerment.

- **Fearlessness and Freedom:** The unapologetic pursuit of their dreams by the women in this chapter serves as a clarion call for others to act fearlessly in the pursuit of their own aspirations.

- **Compassion and Humanity:** Beyond their individual achievements, what sets these women apart is their inherent need to uplift others. Their compassion is as noteworthy as their professional success.

CHAPTER 10

THE JOURNEY TOWARDS A BEAUTIFUL FUTURE

"In every woman's heart lies the power to lead, inspire, and transform the world around her."

– Indira Gandhi

Visualize a garden in full flourish. Each flower, unique in its beauty, stands tall and proud, complementing its neighbor and contributing to the allure of the whole. This garden is a symbol of the collective strength and beauty women bring to the table.

Like every bloom, every woman adds a distinct hue, fragrance, and resilience to the garden of leadership. Together, we cultivate a world where growth is abundant, where ideas flourish, and where dreams blossom into realities.

Our journey towards sculpting a brighter, more equitable future has its roots in a rich past, nurtured by countless women who dared to challenge the norm. We have inherited the legacy of icons like Ruth Bader Ginsburg, who stood tall in her pursuit of justice; Angela

Merkel, who steered with wisdom and poise; and Kamala Harris, who broke barriers with sheer grit and grace.

Drawing inspiration from these legends, we add our brushstrokes to this ever-evolving canvas of women's leadership.

Our stories are the colors that breathe life into this narrative, inspiring others to create their masterpieces. For instance, a tale of a mother teaching her daughter about courage captures the essence of our journey. She said, "Bravery is not the absence of fear but the audacity to act in its face." It's a sentiment each of us should etch into our hearts.

Certainly, our journey is not devoid of challenges. Just as rivers face obstacles, altering their course but never their destination, we too face hurdles. Yet, it's our perseverance, our unyielding spirit that shapes history.

We must always remember that our influence, much like the gentle waves in a pond, has a far-reaching impact. The smallest act of kindness, mentorship, or advocacy creates ripples of change, testament to the enduring power of leadership.

The real essence of leadership lies in the nuances, the everyday acts of courage. Whether it's standing up against prejudice in casual conversations, mentoring a colleague, or driving change in boardrooms - every act counts.

As women, our responsibility extends beyond our personal aspirations. It stretches out to every girl, every woman who aspires to challenge, inspire, and lead. Sharing our tales, our triumphs, and our tribulations, we pave the path for others to follow.

With every step we take, we inch closer to a world that recognizes potential beyond gender, dreams beyond biases, and leadership beyond titles. This mission may be arduous, but the collective strength of women across the globe ensures that no challenge is too daunting.

Let us remember that leadership is not a destination; it's a journey. A journey marked by evolution, resilience, and purpose. To every woman reading this – hold that torch high, for its light guides the way for countless others. Remember, our future, molded by unity, perseverance, and love, awaits our touch. Let's embark on this journey with determination, forging paths where none exist, and painting a future that's equitable, vibrant, and utterly beautiful.

Embrace Your Unique Self: Authenticity is Power

In the vast tapestry of humanity, every individual thread has its own shade, texture, and pattern. When each thread acknowledges and showcases its unique beauty, the entire tapestry becomes a mesmerizing work of art.

Likewise, when you embrace your true self, you not only enrich your own life but also add vibrancy to the world around you.

Each woman we spoke to shared tales of transformation, lessons of resilience, and insights born from personal experiences. One recurring theme was the immense power that lay in being authentic. Shedding the weights of societal pressures and stepping into one's true essence revealed strength and clarity previously unrealized.

One interviewee, a schoolteacher, recalled her days of hiding her passion for dance, thinking it to be a frivolous pursuit amidst her academic responsibilities. Yet, when she integrated dance into her teaching methodologies, not only did her students become more engaged, but she felt a resurgence of energy and passion in her career. She wasn't just teaching subjects; she was teaching life lessons through movement. Her authenticity not only changed the dynamic of her classroom but deeply impacted the lives of her students.

There's an unparalleled beauty in authenticity. It's the courage to stand apart in a crowd, to own your truths even when they diverge from the norm. It's about understanding that your differences aren't deficiencies; they are your defining attributes.

The universe didn't create you to blend in; it crafted you to stand out, to contribute a unique voice to the symphony of existence.

But this journey of authenticity isn't always easy. It requires self-reflection, courage, and often, going against the tide. It's about silencing the external cacophony to listen to the whispers of your heart. And when you do, you'll find that these whispers turn into affirmations, guiding you toward a life filled with purpose and joy.

It's important to cherish your idiosyncrasies, your quirks, your passions, and your dreams. Wear them with pride. Because in the authenticity of your being, you possess an unmatched superpower. When you embrace your unique self, you become an unstoppable force, a beacon of inspiration, and a testament to the limitless potential that authenticity holds. Remember always, your authenticity is your legacy. Celebrate it. Embrace it. Live it.

Understanding Who You Are

Life is often described as a vast, open-ended journey, punctuated with moments of clarity, challenge, and transformation. Of all its twists and turns, perhaps the most rewarding path one can traverse is the inner one— the exploration into the very depths of one's soul.

It's akin to unfolding the pages of a book where every chapter holds revelations about who you truly are and what you're destined to become.

It's interesting to note that our external world, bustling with noise and distractions, can often drown out our internal narratives. The expectations of society, family, and peer groups might set predefined paths for us, creating a blueprint of what our life "should" look like. And in trying to fit into these molds, we might temporarily lose sight of our authentic selves.

The women we connected with beautifully illustrated the myriad ways in which personal discovery can manifest. Their stories weren't just about realizing their true passions or challenging familial expectations, but they also highlighted the quieter, subtler moments of clarity. Like the realization of one's own values, the understanding of one's boundaries, or the gentle acknowledgment of one's own needs and desires.

Another interviewee, a former corporate lawyer, shared her story of taking a sabbatical to travel and volunteer in remote villages. During this time, she discovered her deep connection with nature and sustainable living. She returned not just with photographs, but with a renewed sense of purpose.

Today, she runs an eco-friendly venture and educates people on sustainable practices.

Such stories underline the transformative potential that self-discovery holds. It's about shedding layers of external influences and diving deep within, to find that inner voice which has been whispering all along. The beauty of this journey is that it's never truly over; as we evolve and grow, we continually discover newer facets of our being.

So, as you embark on or continue this inward voyage, remember to be gentle with yourself. Cherish every revelation, be it big or small, and honor the journey, with all its highs and lows. Because in understanding who you are, you unlock a world of possibilities, not just for yourself but for all those whose lives you touch. And in that profound understanding, lies the true essence of living.

Embracing Your Flaws and Strengths

Life is a delicate balance of light and shadows. Just as the most beautiful art pieces are given depth and dimension through a dance of contrasts, our lives are made richer and more textured by our strengths and our flaws. Authenticity doesn't demand perfection; rather, it celebrates the full spectrum of our being.

In embracing both our radiant strengths and our vulnerable imperfections, we become embodiments of genuine humanity.

The women we interviewed echoed this sentiment profoundly. One shared, "It was only when I accepted my flaws that I truly began to understand my strengths. They were two sides of the same coin." Another revealed, "I used to hide behind a façade of perfection. But once I let my guard down and showed the world my true self, flaws and all, I found a deeper connection with those around me."

The idea of being "flawed" often carries negative connotations in today's culture, where curated lives on social media platforms can create an illusion of seamless perfection. However, our flaws, our imperfections, our scars—they give testimony to our journeys, our battles, our resilience, and our growth. They show that we have faced challenges and emerged stronger, wiser, and more attuned to our own worth.

Conversely, our strengths are the compass points, guiding us, propelling us forward, and helping us make a positive impact on the world. They're our superpowers, unique to each individual, and they shine brightly, illuminating the path for ourselves and others.

Accenture's survey offers empirical validation to what many have felt intuitively: authenticity, with all its intricate interplay of strengths and flaws, is a cornerstone of success. It's about recognizing that our vulnerabilities don't diminish our value; they enhance it. They make our successes more meaningful and our stories more compelling.

In a world that often seems to value conformity, dare to be unapologetically you. Embrace every facet of your being—the brilliance and the blemishes. For in that embrace, you'll find freedom, connection, and a deep, resonant sense of purpose. Remember, it's the mosaic of our strengths and flaws that create the beautiful masterpiece that is each one of us..

Living Your Truth

There's a deep-rooted magic that comes from living in alignment with one's truth. It is akin to finding your inner compass, which consistently points you towards genuine fulfillment and purpose. Every decision, every action, every word spoken is a reflection of the essence of who you are, an embodiment of your core values and beliefs.

In a world replete with fleeting trends, external pressures, and the constant hum of others' opinions, the commitment to live your truth can sometimes feel like swimming against the current.

But those who dare to embrace this authenticity often find that the journey, though challenging, is deeply rewarding.

The women we spoke to reiterated this sentiment. A nonprofit founder shared, "The moment I started living my truth, everything changed. It was as if I had tuned into a frequency that was uniquely mine. Decisions became clearer, my relationships deepened, and I found a sense of peace I had never known."

Research by the Center for Creative Leadership underscores the profound impact of authenticity in leadership roles. Leaders who live their truth, who present themselves genuinely and transparently, cultivate environments where trust and respect thrive. When a leader is genuine, it breaks down barriers, paving the way for open communication, collaboration, and innovation. It empowers teams, fostering a culture where individuals feel valued and heard. This, in turn, translates to enhanced organizational performance, higher employee engagement, and a workplace culture that is both inclusive and dynamic.

Living your truth is not just a personal endeavor; it's a leadership strategy. It's about recognizing and honoring the immense power that comes from being unapologetically you.

In doing so, you not only illuminate your own path but also light the way for others, inspiring them to discover and embrace their authentic selves.

So, as you navigate the vast tapestry of life, remember the words of Shakespeare: "To thine own self be true." For in that truth lies the power to transform, inspire, and lead with unparalleled impact.

Creating a Safe Space for Others

In a world where so many wear masks, where facades are often more valued than authenticity, being true to oneself is an act of courage. And it's a courage that doesn't go unnoticed. By fully embodying your true self, you unknowingly send out an invitation, a silent beckoning, for others to do the same.

Your authenticity acts as a lighthouse in the murky waters of societal expectations, guiding others towards their own shores of genuine self-expression. It tells them, "Here is a space where you can be you, unapologetically and without judgment." This safe haven, birthed from your authenticity, fosters an environment where vulnerability is embraced, and masks can be shed.

Consider the impact of such spaces. The magic that unfolds when people let down their guards, allowing their souls to breathe freely, to engage in conversations that matter, and to form connections that run deep and true. It's like creating a sanctuary where human spirits can thrive, unencumbered by the weight of pretense.

One woman, a community leader, shared her perspective: "By being myself, flaws and all, I saw walls crumble and conversations flourish. People came forward with their stories, their dreams, and their fears. It was as if my authenticity had given them a key to unlock their own."

Your authentic self not only sets you free but creates ripples, touching hearts and souls, catalyzing a chain reaction of genuine self-expression. In being truly you, you not only elevate your own life but also pave the way for others to find their voice, their truth, and their sanctuary in the world.

So, as you journey through life with your authentic flag flying high, know that you're doing more than just living your truth. You're creating spaces, nurturing environments, and fostering communities where authenticity is not just welcomed but celebrated.

A Lifelong Journey

In the hustle and bustle of life, amidst the swirling tides of societal expectations and the cacophony of external voices, it is easy to lose oneself.

Yet, as the stories of countless women unveiled, understanding and embracing oneself is not a singular event but an enduring expedition. It's akin to a river that continuously carves its path, sometimes gently and sometimes with fervor, but always with purpose.

One of the women, a poet by profession, shared a profound reflection, "Just when I thought I knew myself, life introduced me to a version of me I hadn't met. It's like reading a book where every chapter reveals a new facet, a deeper understanding." This metaphor beautifully encapsulates the essence of the lifelong journey of self-discovery.

As humans, we are not static beings. Our experiences, encounters, challenges, and triumphs continuously shape us. Each day brings new lessons, and with them, new aspects of ourselves waiting to be uncovered. It's a never-ending dance of understanding, acceptance, and growth.

A renowned psychologist once said, "The journey of self-discovery is the most important journey we can take, yet it's also the most overlooked." In a world so fixated on external achievements, it's crucial to remember that internal growth holds an unmatched depth and significance.

A young activist we interviewed expressed it aptly, "There were days I felt I had lost myself in the cause. But then, in quiet moments of reflection, I realized that I wasn't losing myself; I was finding newer, stronger versions of me. Each challenge, each setback was but a stepping stone to a deeper understanding of who I am."

In this journey, there will be moments of doubt, of questioning, of rediscovery, and that's perfectly okay. Each phase, each challenge, each epiphany is a stepping stone towards a richer understanding of oneself. The journey is filled with its twists and turns, peaks and troughs, but through it all, it's a beautiful odyssey of becoming.

So, as you traverse this journey of life, remember to continually check in with yourself, to realign, rediscover, and rejoice in the ever-evolving masterpiece that is you. Embrace every moment, every revelation, for this lifelong journey is where the true magic of existence lies.

You Are Enough

In an era where comparison is but a click away, it becomes increasingly challenging to embrace one's essence fully. Yet, among the narratives shared by women leaders, a resonant theme emerged: the empowerment derived from understanding that 'you are enough'. Each interview painted a vivid tableau of personal stories, challenges, victories, and lessons. But a common thread that wove these tales together was the acknowledgment and celebration of their unique selves.

An environmental activist we spoke to reflected on her journey, "For years, I tried to emulate leaders I admired, but it left me exhausted. The moment I embraced my own way of leading, rooted in my values and strengths, I started resonating with people in ways I'd never imagined."

This sentiment is not isolated. A groundbreaking study by McKinsey & Company underscored that authentic leadership – characterized by self-awareness, transparency, and integrity – contributes to a more engaged workforce and stronger organizational performance. When leaders lead with authenticity, it fosters an environment where others feel seen, valued, and empowered to bring their whole selves to work.

However, reaching this realization of 'enoughness' is a journey. A tech entrepreneur shared, "Every pitch, every boardroom, I'd enter with the weight of trying to be someone else. It took me failing and rebuilding to recognize that my unique perspective was my asset. The tech world didn't need another version of an existing leader; it needed me."

This belief in oneself, in one's uniqueness, is transformative. It isn't about ego, but about understanding that each individual offers a unique perspective, a singular blend of experiences, and a distinct voice. And in that uniqueness lies the ability to connect, inspire, and lead in unparalleled ways.

So, to every woman reading this, remember: Your individuality is not a deviation from the norm, but a beautiful divergence that has the potential to forge new paths, inspire new thinking, and lead with unparalleled authenticity. In a world filled with molds, your distinct shape has the power to redefine leadership paradigms. Stand tall, lead with heart, and always remember: You are more than enough.

Live Your Passion

Heartfelt Decisions Lead the Way

The ember of passion within can warm not only one's own heart but can blaze a trail for many to follow. To live a life fueled by passion is to wake up each morning with purpose, with fire in your veins, and a yearning to make a mark.

Many women we interviewed echoed this sentiment, highlighting how anchoring their decisions in passion led to richer, more fulfilling experiences. One entrepreneur shared, "Every venture I started came from an itch in my soul. Some succeeded, some failed, but each was a labor of love and taught me more than any 'safe' job ever could."

Passion, when intertwined with daily life and

decisions, becomes more than just a feeling; it's a compass. It directs choices, propels action, and offers solace in challenging times. One educator told us, "Every time I felt overwhelmed, I thought of the spark in my students' eyes, my passion for teaching. That kept me going, even on the toughest days."

The influence of passion goes beyond the individual. As the Deloitte study underscores, passion-driven leadership doesn't just motivate the leader; it creates a domino effect. Teams are more inspired, workplaces become more vibrant, and the mission of an organization transforms from a statement on paper to a lived experience.

Moreover, living one's passion creates a mosaic of authentic stories, stories that inspire others to find their own paths. A renowned dancer we interviewed poetically said, "Every step I took on stage wasn't just a dance move; it was a narrative of my passion. And I hope it encourages others to write their own stories."

From our conversations, it became evident that living with passion is not a whimsical choice. It's a conscious decision to align one's heart, mind, and actions. It's about embracing vulnerability, taking risks, and most importantly, staying true to oneself. After all, as many of our interviewees affirmed, when you tread the path of passion, even challenges become beautiful dances of growth and transformation.

Discovering Your Passion

In the relentless pace of life, pausing to introspect and ask oneself, "What genuinely excites me?" is a luxury few afford themselves. Yet, as our interviews have shown, this introspection can be the compass leading to a life of deeper fulfillment and purpose.

The path to discovering one's passion is seldom linear. It's filled with twists and turns, moments of doubt, and exhilarating revelations. Many women recounted periods of feeling lost, only to stumble upon an interest or activity that would ignite a previously unknown spark within them.

A pediatrician told us, "I always believed medicine was my calling. But a chance involvement in a children's theater workshop made me realize that drama was my true passion. Now, I integrate theater techniques into my sessions with children, making the healing process more interactive and therapeutic."

Discovering one's passion often requires a mix of introspection, experimentation, and openness. For some, it's about revisiting childhood interests that were left behind in the pursuit of practicality. For others, it might be exploring entirely new avenues, taking courses, attending workshops, or simply being more observant about what brings them joy in daily life.

Another woman, a lawyer by training, found her passion in pottery. "The first time I touched clay, there was an indescribable connection. The rigidity of my professional life melted away with the malleability of the clay. It became my escape, my meditation, and eventually, my vocation."

These stories also highlight the transformative power of passion. When one finds what they truly love, it's not just about personal joy or a career shift. It has a ripple effect, influencing the communities they're part of. Their enthusiasm becomes contagious, inspiring others to seek out and follow their own passions.

For those still on the quest to discover their passion, the women we interviewed offered a collective piece of wisdom: Be patient, stay curious, and trust the journey. The pursuit itself, with its trials and triumphs, is as enriching as the final revelation. And when that revelation comes, it has the power to illuminate not just one's path but to light up the world in its unique glow.

Aligning Passion with Profession

The intersection of passion and profession is a

coveted sweet spot for many. When what we love aligns with what we do for a living, it transforms the very nature of 'work'. Instead of a series of tasks, work becomes a platform for expression, innovation, and impact.

Throughout our interviews, it became evident that women who had aligned their passions with their professions were not only more satisfied but also more influential in their respective fields. Their enthusiasm was infectious, often inspiring colleagues, subordinates, and even superiors.

A teacher we interviewed mentioned, "When I began teaching, it was just a job. But the moment I realized that my passion for storytelling could make history come alive for my students, everything changed. My classrooms became more interactive, students more engaged, and I found joy in every lecture."

There's an undeniable energy that emanates from someone who loves what they do. This energy often translates into innovation, as passionate professionals are always looking for ways to improve, adapt, and grow. They're not just driven by paychecks or promotions; they're driven by purpose and the deep-seated satisfaction of contributing meaningfully.

However, aligning passion with profession isn't always straightforward. It might involve lateral moves, further education, or even starting from scratch in a new field. One woman we spoke with recounted her journey from finance to wildlife photography. "I was climbing the corporate ladder, but something felt amiss. On a trip to Africa, I discovered my passion for wildlife photography. Making the switch was daunting, but today, I wouldn't trade it for anything. Every photograph tells a story, and I'm honored to share those stories with the world."

For some, aligning passion with profession means molding their current job to better fit their interests. For others, it might mean starting a side venture or hobby that complements their day job. The key is to be open to possibilities, to be curious, and to actively seek opportunities that allow your passion to shine.

Ultimately, when passion and profession come together, it creates a synergy that benefits not just the individual but the entire ecosystem they're a part of. Organizations thrive, communities benefit, and individuals find a deeper sense of fulfillment, knowing that every day they're not just working, but they're making a difference doing what they love.

The Courage to Follow Your Heart

When the heart speaks, it conveys a truth that the mind might struggle to understand. Following this voice, especially when the world tries to drown it out, demands a rare kind of bravery. Our interviews with numerous women revealed time and time again the immense courage they summoned to pursue their passions, often against considerable odds.

There's a societal blueprint many feel compelled to follow: a 'safe' job, a predictable routine, the familiar, and the tried-and-tested. But the heart, with its dreams and aspirations, often tugs in another direction. The path it suggests may be laden with uncertainties, challenges, and naysayers questioning every step. And yet, it promises fulfillment, joy, and a life lived with purpose.

An entrepreneur we spoke to recalled her journey saying, "Everyone thought I was mad to leave a high-paying job to start my own venture. There were days I doubted myself too, days when everything seemed to go wrong. But every time I felt the joy of doing what I loved, every time a customer's face lit up, I was reminded of why I took this path."

This courage isn't about being reckless or impulsive. It's about listening intently to that inner voice, weighing the pros and cons, and then taking a leap of faith, believing in one's abilities and the inherent goodness of the universe to support genuine endeavors.

Many women emphasized the initial fears they felt— the fear of failure, judgment, or even success. But they also spoke of the exhilaration of breaking through those fears. One artist put it beautifully, "Every brushstroke was a challenge, a confrontation with my own insecurities. But when the canvas finally reflected my vision, every fear melted away."

One of the most powerful lessons these stories teach us is that courage isn't a grand, one-time act. It's a daily choice. It's choosing to show up every day, even when the going gets tough. It's trusting that even if things don't go as planned, the journey itself will be worth it. And more often than not, when one musters the courage to follow their heart, serendipity steps in, doors open, and the universe truly does conspire to make their dreams come true.

Passion as a Catalyst for Change

When one's heart is deeply invested in a cause or pursuit, it radiates an energy that's palpable, contagious even. Such passion transcends the personal realm and becomes a force that can reshape communities, industries, and even societal norms. In our conversations, we found that women who led with passion became not just successful individuals, but transformative agents who reshaped the world in their unique ways.

Imagine a stone thrown into a pond, creating ripples that spread far and wide. Similarly, a passionate endeavor doesn't just benefit the individual; its influence ripples out, touching lives, motivating peers, and sparking innovation. The vibrant energy and commitment of passionate individuals serve as powerful testimonials to the idea that with enough dedication and zeal, any barrier can be transcended, any vision realized.

One environmental activist we interviewed narrated her journey saying, "When I started, it was just about saving a small patch of forest near my home. But as my passion grew, so did the movement. Today, we're not just saving forests, but transforming the way entire cities think about green spaces."

Furthermore, passionate leaders infuse their organizations with a culture of dynamism, resilience, and creativity. They are often at the forefront of groundbreaking initiatives and inspire their teams to push boundaries and envision greater possibilities. The Deloitte report corroborates this, highlighting how such leaders leverage their passion to foster environments where innovation thrives and challenges are seen not as setbacks but as opportunities for growth.

But perhaps the most profound impact of living one's passion is the message it sends to the younger generation. It tells them that the pursuit of one's dreams is not just a romantic notion, but a viable, rewarding path. As a teacher in our series remarked, "When my students see me excited about a subject, they don't just learn the topic. They learn to love learning."

In essence, passion, when wielded with intention and purpose, is more than just a personal compass. It's a transformative tool, a beacon that illuminates the path for others, and most importantly, a testament to the profound change one individual's fervor can bring about in the world.

Nurturing Your Passion

To live a life driven by passion is like sailing on a sea with ever-changing tides and winds. While the direction and force of these elements can change, a seasoned sailor knows how to adjust the sails and harness the winds to keep moving forward. Similarly, nurturing one's passion is about making constant adjustments, refining one's approach, and ensuring the fire within remains undimmed.

Throughout our interviews, women echoed this sentiment with tales that wove together challenges, breakthroughs, and reaffirmations of their chosen path. Their stories served as gentle reminders that while the initial spark of passion is innate, keeping it alive requires effort, intention, and, sometimes, a bit of reinvention.

One photographer we spoke with shed light on her journey, saying, "There were periods when the world looked monochrome, devoid of the vibrant colors I so loved capturing. But in those moments, I learned to see differently, to find beauty in shadows and patterns, to nurture my passion in ways I hadn't before."

The act of nurturing involves consistent engagement with your craft. It's about seeking out opportunities to deepen your understanding and evolve in your expression.

It might involve learning from others who have walked the path before you, immersing yourself in environments that stimulate your creativity, or even stepping back when needed to rekindle the flame from a distance.

Moreover, the environment and company you keep play pivotal roles. Surrounding oneself with supportive, understanding, and equally passionate individuals can make the difference between a fleeting interest and a lifelong pursuit. As an author in our series shared, "Every chapter of my life was written not just by me, but by the collective wisdom and encouragement of those who believed in my story."

Ultimately, to nurture your passion is to honor the very essence of who you are, to commit to a journey of authenticity, and to remember that even on days when the path seems obscured, the destination — a life led with passion — is worth every step.

Your Passion is Your Purpose

Amid the noise of societal expectations, relentless pursuit of material goals, and the external pressures to fit certain molds, one's genuine passion often stands as a beacon of authenticity. It's not just a fleeting interest or a temporary infatuation; it's an intrinsic part of who you are. It's the symphony that resonates with your soul, urging you to break free from the ordinary and dive deep into the realms of your genuine self.

Numerous women we've conversed with have embodied this truth in awe-inspiring ways. These are women who have transformed their passions into powerful vehicles for change, breaking boundaries, and redefining paradigms.

A seasoned chef who turned her passion for food into a culinary school for underprivileged children shared, "Food was always my solace. But over time, I realized it was my conduit to empower, to educate, and to elevate lives. Every dish I teach is not just a recipe; it's a life lesson."

Passion is the bedrock upon which lasting legacies are built. It's the force that drives you to work long hours, face daunting challenges head-on, and still wake up every morning with that same zeal. More importantly, a life driven by passion stands as a testament, not just to personal success but to a life infused with meaning and purpose.

An environmental activist emphasized, "Every time I see a tree being saved or a policy being revised, I feel a sense of triumph. It's not about the accolades; it's about living my truth and knowing I'm doing something bigger than myself."

It's crucial to comprehend that passion transcends the spectrum of grand achievements. It manifests in the everyday, in the mundane, and in the quiet moments. Perhaps it's in the way a mother shares stories with her children, in the melodies a young girl composes in her room, or in the dedication of a teacher who goes beyond textbooks to inspire minds.

A writer who discovered her love for storytelling in her late 40s revealed, "It was never about becoming a bestseller. It was about connecting, touching hearts, and knowing that my stories might offer solace, insight, or simply a moment of joy."

In an age where metrics often define success, let your passion be your most authentic measure. Embrace it, nurture it, and allow it to guide you. For in doing so, you not only enrich your life but inspire countless others. Your passion is more than just a calling; it's your legacy. And remember, when passion meets purpose, the results are nothing short of magical.

Redefine Possible

Your Limitations are Only in Your Mind

The women we interviewed conveyed a profound truth: often, the barriers we perceive are constructs forged by our own beliefs and past experiences. Their stories, spanning diverse backgrounds and industries, harmonized around a shared theme – the transformative power of self-belief and the audacity to redefine boundaries.

Fueled by dreams and ambitions, these women confronted doubters, skeptics, and more crucially, the internal echoes of generations' worth of conditioning regarding what women "should" or "shouldn't" pursue. Yet, woven through each narrative was a pivotal mindset shift.

A young entrepreneur from a rural setting shared, "In my village, women didn't run businesses. But every time I sold handmade crafts, I realized my potential wasn't confined by where I came from. Today, I helm a thriving e-commerce platform, showcasing crafts from the remotest corners of our nation."

The Harvard Business Review study reiterates an essential facet of these stories. By dismantling barriers, these women were not just achieving personal triumphs; they were becoming crucibles for innovation. By defying conventions, they introduced fresh perspectives, novel solutions, and an invigorating dynamism to their fields.

A CEO from a leading fintech firm reflected, "When I ventured into fintech, it felt like an exclusive domain. Every seminar, every conference, I was in the minority. But that distinction became my strength. My unique approach to challenges paved the way for innovative solutions and, eventually, pioneering breakthroughs."

However, redefining what's possible isn't limited to monumental accomplishments. It's reflected in daily acts of bravery – taking the floor in a meeting, delving into an unconventional hobby, standing up for oneself, or the audacity to dream beyond societal confines.

A schoolteacher offered a heartwarming revelation, "Every day, I assure my students, especially the girls, that their aspirations are valid. It's a small gesture, but I'm convinced that these seeds of affirmation could someday lead them to usher in transformative changes."

To encapsulate, redefining what's possible is a relentless voyage. It beckons us to challenge, to question, and above all, to trust in our capabilities. It is a clarion call to each individual to recognize that most limitations are self-imposed. In transcending these, we not only discover our boundless potential but also light the path for countless others.

Our conversations with hundreds of women unveiled a recurring and potent theme: the power to redefine what's possible and transcend self-imposed limitations. These weren't mere words; they were lived experiences, shared wisdom, and heartfelt insights from women across different walks of life. Here's what we learned:

Breaking Free from Societal Expectations

The weight of societal expectations can often be suffocating. These expectations can be rooted in age-old traditions, cultural norms, or stereotypical beliefs about gender roles. For many women, this manifests as an invisible cage, confining their dreams, aspirations, and even their sense of self. But as our interviews showcased, these chains, however strong, can be broken.

One recurring sentiment among the women was the realization that societal expectations were not just external pressures but often internalized beliefs. They had grown up hearing, absorbing, and sometimes even accepting what they "should" be doing, how they "should" be behaving, and what they "should" be aspiring to.

Breaking free, then, was not just a physical or external act but a profound internal transformation.

An educator who chose not to have children remarked, "For the longest time, I believed that motherhood was the pinnacle of a woman's life. When I realized that wasn't my calling, the backlash was intense. But I also learned that my worth wasn't tied to societal definitions. I carved out a different kind of nurturing role, molding minds in the classroom."

Stories poured in from women who had defied norms, be it in their career choices, personal decisions, or lifestyle. From women who chose solo travel adventures over settled lives, to those who ventured into fields predominantly occupied by men, to women who pushed back against age-related stereotypes, each narrative was a testament to courage and self-belief.

A septuagenarian triathlete told us, "People kept telling me I was too old. That I should be taking it easy. But why? I felt alive when I ran, swam, and cycled. I wasn't going to let age or societal norms dictate my passion."

But breaking free wasn't always about grand gestures or radical changes. For many, it was subtle, quiet decisions – choosing authenticity over approval, prioritizing self-care over self-sacrifice, or simply allowing oneself the freedom to dream differently.

An architect-turned-chef shared her journey, "I was at the pinnacle of my architectural career, but I yearned for something different. I loved cooking. Transitioning wasn't easy; the skepticism was palpable. But every time I plate a dish today, I'm reminded of the beauty of following one's heart, even if it leads you down an unexpected path."

The overarching theme in all these stories was an innate desire to redefine success on one's own terms. These women, in rejecting conformity, were not just challenging societal norms; they were inviting others to question, reflect, and find their own liberating truths.

In the words of the tech leader who transitioned from a traditional role, finding one's path is indeed liberating. But more than that, it's a journey of self-discovery, a proclamation of individuality, and a beacon for countless others who aspire to break free from the molds society imposes upon them.

Growth Mindset in Action

The idea of possessing a growth mindset has gained significant traction in recent years, propounded as the philosophy of embracing challenges and viewing failures not as evidence of unintelligence but as a springboard for growth and stretching existing abilities. However, it's one thing to speak about a growth mindset in the abstract and another to see it manifested in daily lives.

Our interviews illuminated the latter, showcasing how embodying a growth mindset was often the difference between giving up and pushing forward.

For many women we spoke to, life wasn't about arriving at a destination but about savoring the journey, with its myriad experiences – both bitter and sweet. It was about understanding that while expertise is an outcome, the process of getting there is filled with trials, errors, and invaluable learning.

A seasoned academic remarked, "In my early years, every research setback felt devastating. Over time, I realized these were not dead-ends but detours, pointing me towards newer, uncharted territories of knowledge."

This embrace of the 'learning curve' was seen across fields. From startups to arts, women were applying the growth mindset to their challenges, transforming hurdles into opportunities. It wasn't about denying the pain of setbacks but about reframing them, seeing them as a vital part of personal and professional evolution.

A renowned artist shared, "Every critique on my work initially felt like a blow. But then, I started seeing them as doorways to refinement. Each piece of feedback, positive or negative, was a brushstroke on my canvas of growth."

The recurring theme was the belief in adaptability

and the potential for development. The women believed in their capacity to evolve, to change, and to grow, regardless of age, experience, or background.

A senior corporate leader reflected, "In my 40s, I had to adapt to the digital age. I could've seen it as a challenge too steep, but I viewed it as a new adventure. Today, I'm leading digital transformations, all because I believed I wasn't static but ever-evolving."

The story of the young entrepreneur, navigating the labyrinth of business with the compass of a growth mindset, encapsulates the essence of this philosophy. Every stumble is not a fall but a chance to rise stronger, every uncertainty not a pitfall but a potential for discovery, and every challenge not an impediment but an invitation to innovate.

In a world that often celebrates outcomes, these women were a reminder that the journey is just as important. It's in the journey, with its highs and lows, that we find ourselves, redefine our boundaries, and truly understand the power of a growth mindset in action.

The Importance of Mentorship and Community

In the mosaic of experiences that shape our journeys, few elements stand out as profoundly as mentorship and the embrace of a supportive community. Time and again, throughout our interviews, we heard heartwarming tales of guidance, affirmation, and empowerment, highlighting the transformative impact of having someone believe in you and a community to back you up.

Mentorship, as narrated by these women, transcended the traditional notion of mere guidance. It was about forging connections, challenging preconceptions, and expanding horizons. Mentors were not just advisors; they were visionaries who identified latent potential, advocates who tirelessly championed their mentees, and pillars of strength in moments of doubt.

One young entrepreneur recounted, "When I was riddled with self-doubt, my mentor reminded me of my strengths. Her belief in me became the anchor I needed during turbulent times." Such is the power of mentorship – it provides clarity amidst confusion, instills confidence amidst insecurity, and offers direction amidst disarray.

On the flip side, mentors often spoke of the reciprocal nature of these relationships. The act of mentoring was as enlightening for them as it was for their mentees. It presented opportunities to reflect, learn, and grow alongside those they guided. As one seasoned professional put it, "Mentoring kept me grounded. In helping others navigate their paths, I often found insights into my own journey."

Parallel to mentorship is the indispensable role of community. Communities, be they professional networks, friend groups, or broader societal circles, serve as reservoirs of collective wisdom, encouragement, and resilience. Women emphasized how, within these spaces, they found camaraderie, shared challenges, celebrated successes, and most importantly, felt a sense of belonging.

A startup founder expressed, "In my toughest moments, it was my community that rallied around me, offering resources, connections, and unwavering support. They were the safety net I didn't even know I had."

The synergy between mentorship and community is evident. While mentors provide focused guidance and direction, communities offer broad-based support and resources. Together, they create an ecosystem that nurtures, empowers, and propels individuals forward.

The sentiment encapsulated by the executive, reflecting on the transformative influence of her mentor, is a testament to the profound potential of these relationships. It underscores the fact that sometimes, all one needs is for someone to see in them what they fail to see in themselves. And when that insight is coupled with the strength of a community, the boundaries of what's possible expand exponentially.

In this nurturing environment, dreams take flight, potentials are realized, and legacies are born.

Calculated Risks and Courage

The journey to success and fulfillment often requires a departure from the familiar, venturing into the unknown. Throughout our discussions, the motif of calculated risks resounded strongly, illuminating the paths taken by countless women who dared to step beyond the realm of comfort and certainty. They spoke of moments where decisions weighed heavily, of times when the familiar beckoned enticingly, but the promise of what lay beyond was too compelling to ignore.

These were not just impulsive decisions. They were the result of introspection, meticulous planning, and a deep understanding of one's capabilities and aspirations. Such decisions, while fraught with uncertainty, were rooted in a conviction that stemmed from self-awareness and a desire to realize a larger vision. These women recognized that every risk carries the potential for both failure and unparalleled reward. But more than the outcome, it was the journey, the process of overcoming challenges and growing from them, that held intrinsic value.

One entrepreneur recalled, "Starting my own business meant leaving behind a steady paycheck and stepping into the unpredictable. But it also meant waking up every day with a passion, knowing that I was building something of my own." This sentiment was echoed by many, highlighting the profound satisfaction that comes from pursuing one's passion, even in the face of adversity.

Another element that shone through these tales of risk-taking was the sheer courage it required. Courage to defy societal norms, to face naysayers, to endure setbacks, and to continue pushing forward with unwavering determination. This courage was not about the absence of fear but about acting despite it.

The nonprofit leader's story serves as a poignant reminder of the ripple effect that one courageous decision can create.

Taking the risk to follow her heart did not just alter the trajectory of her life, but it resonated outwards, touching and transforming countless others. "Every risk I took," she reflected, "wasn't just about me. It was about the communities I wanted to serve, the lives I hoped to touch."

The narratives around calculated risks and courage underscore a profound truth: while the path of risk is paved with challenges and uncertainties, it is also where the most transformative journeys occur. And for the women who walk this path, armed with conviction, courage, and clarity, the rewards – both tangible and intangible – are immeasurable.

The Collective Wisdom

Throughout our interviews, a vivid panorama of grit, passion, and boundless aspirations emerged. Each woman brought her unique narrative to the table, creating a chorus of experiences that spoke of both individual triumphs and shared victories. These tales of perseverance weren't isolated instances; they represented a collective symphony of empowered voices echoing through time.

This amalgamation of wisdom showcases not just personal achievements but reflects a shared journey through the labyrinth of societal expectations, personal challenges, and the quest for self-actualization. Every story we heard illuminated the multifaceted strength inherent in women, emphasizing the vast reservoir of potential that lies within. It became evident that this collective wisdom isn't just about personal experiences but is an age-old legacy passed down through generations.

More than ever, it's essential to recognize that these shared tales are not mere footnotes in the annals of history. They are the very essence of a burgeoning revolution, a dynamic force propelling us forward. With each story of a woman breaking barriers, defying norms, or simply making a choice that aligns with her true self, the narrative of what's possible expands. It is this ever-expanding horizon that beckons to every individual, urging them to step beyond convention, reach for the stars, and forge their unique path.

But the power of these stories doesn't stop with individual inspiration. They form a rich tapestry of interconnected lives, symbolizing the collective power of unity. These narratives become the building blocks of a global movement, championing the values of empowerment, determination, and visionary leadership. They send a resonating message: No dream is too vast, no ambition too high when we stand together, pooling our wisdom and resources.

In this collective wisdom lies a profound responsibility: to not only honor the lessons from these narratives but to pass them on, amplifying their impact. Each story, each voice, serves as a torchbearer for the coming generation, lighting the way and dispelling shadows of doubt and fear.

So, as we reflect upon these tales of tenacity and vision, let us remember that they are more than motivational accounts. They are a clarion call, urging us to join hands, embrace our shared legacy, and stride forth into a future where the impossible is merely a challenge awaiting its solution.

Together, fortified by our collective wisdom, we are unstoppable.

Holistic Problem-Solving

Your Everyday Wisdom Shapes the World

Life's intricate web is something women navigate daily with grace and tenacity. From tending to a child's fever while preparing for a crucial board meeting, to aiding a neighbor amidst personal challenges, women are often at the forefront of handling multifaceted situations. The intuition and insights garnered from such experiences make them adept problem solvers, not just at the individual level but for the collective good.

A prime example of this is reflected in the business world. A McKinsey & Company report illuminated that companies boasting diverse leadership, especially including women, are 21% more likely to witness above-average profitability. Why is this so? It's deeply rooted in women's holistic approach to problem-solving, an approach that is cultivated through their daily experiences. This 'bigger picture thinking', an amalgamation of multitasking dexterity and empathetic understanding, uniquely distinguishes their leadership and decision-making styles.

But it's not only in corporate echelons where this

wisdom shines. In our numerous dialogues with women from all walks of life, a profound understanding emerged. Whether they are educators, caregivers, artists, or engineers, their natural inclination is to look beyond the immediate issue, delving into the interconnected roots, causes, and implications. This holistic perspective is not about solving a singular problem, but about understanding its place in a larger system and working towards sustainable, comprehensive solutions.

One environmental activist we interviewed put it succinctly, "When I advocate for cleaner oceans, it's not just about the sea creatures. It's about the fishing communities, the tourism sector, the health of our planet, and our children's future." This interconnected thinking, this ability to discern how one issue weaves into a broader tapestry, is a testament to women's innate problem-solving prowess.

Indeed, as we venture deeper into an age defined by complexity and rapid change, this ability to see the broader canvas and to connect seemingly disparate dots becomes ever more critical. Women, with their holistic insights borne out of their myriad roles and responsibilities, are poised to be the guiding lights, leading us toward a future that is not only more prosperous but also more equitable, balanced, and harmonious.

The Multitasking Mastery

Wisdom in Everyday Life

The narratives that unfolded during our interviews painted a vivid image of the multifaceted lives many women lead. Their ability to manage multiple tasks and roles simultaneously is not just a testament to their efficiency but is deeply rooted in a profound understanding of relationships, systems, and priorities. This aptitude, often labeled as multitasking, goes beyond mere task-juggling. It's a complex dance of decision-making, where choices in one domain reverberate through others, creating harmonies or challenges in their wake.

This "dance" can be seen in the way a professional mom coordinates her work schedule with her child's school activities, ensuring neither sphere is neglected. Or how a woman entrepreneur might align her business decisions with community needs, recognizing that success is richer when it uplifts others. Such daily orchestrations may seem routine or even mundane, but they're a manifestation of an innate skill to perceive, adapt, and create harmony in a world of interdependence.

One mother and business owner encapsulated this sentiment, saying, "Every day, I'm making decisions that impact my family, my business, my community. It's a constant balancing act, but it's taught me to see the bigger picture." These words highlight an important point: multitasking is not merely an operational skill but is grounded in an evolved perspective. This ability to discern how actions in one arena might cascade into another is a form of wisdom, one that has been honed through lived experiences.

Moreover, in their multitasking prowess, women often draw upon a reservoir of emotional intelligence, intuition, and foresight. As another interviewee, a teacher and community volunteer, expressed, "When I'm juggling lessons, community meetings, and my family's needs, it's not just about time management. It's about understanding the emotional and long-term implications of my decisions on my students, my family, and the community."

In celebrating this multitasking mastery, we're not just acknowledging the efficient management of tasks but are recognizing the profound wisdom that many women wield daily. It's about seeing the connections, understanding the ripple effects, and making choices that align with a broader vision of well-being, harmony, and growth.

Thinking Globally

Solutions for the Greater Good

Throughout the journey of uncovering leadership

traits and decision-making dynamics, one standout attribute among the women interviewed was their penchant for a global perspective. This doesn't merely mean thinking about international affairs but refers to an overarching, holistic view, where decisions are gauged not just by their immediate results but by the ripple effects they create, both near and far. The ability to zoom out, see the interconnectedness of systems, and consider the larger narrative is a powerful tool in the arsenal of effective leaders.

One of the underlying reasons for this global thought process is the innate sense of responsibility and stewardship that many women feel towards their communities, environments, and future generations. This vision goes beyond borders, cultures, and immediate timelines. It's about recognizing that our actions today have long-term consequences and being deeply committed to ensuring those outcomes are positive, sustainable, and inclusive.

A nonprofit leader encapsulated this sentiment, saying, "I don't just look at the immediate problem; I look at how solving it will affect the entire community. It's about creating lasting change." Her approach reflects a common theme: the idea of legacy. It's not about quick fixes or isolated successes; it's about laying the groundwork for a future that continues to benefit from today's actions.

Another entrepreneur in sustainable technologies mentioned, "When I think of a product, I'm not just considering its immediate market potential. I contemplate its environmental footprint, the societal shifts it might foster, and how it can be part of a more sustainable future." Such perspectives reveal a profound understanding of interconnected systems and a dedication to ensuring that progress in one area doesn't come at the detriment of another.

In a world that can often feel fragmented, where problems seem insurmountable due to their vast and complex nature, this global thinking is a beacon of hope. It reminds us that with the right perspective, every challenge can be an opportunity to effect change that resonates beyond our immediate environment, reaching out to touch communities, ecosystems, and generations yet unborn. It's a call to rise above the myopic and strive for solutions that truly serve the greater good.

Empathy and Compassion

The Heart of Problem-Solving

In the whirlwind of strategy sessions, brainstorming, and search for cutting-edge solutions, the interviews revealed a more profound, human-centric truth: the core of genuine problem-solving lies in empathy and compassion. These two virtues aren't just pleasant additives; they are foundational to understanding the multi-faceted dimensions of an issue and tailoring solutions that address root causes, not just surface-level symptoms.

Empathy, the ability to step into another's shoes and see the world through their eyes, gives a depth of insight that no data or analytics can offer. It allows us to perceive the emotional, psychological, and sometimes hidden aspects of a situation. Compassion, on the other hand, is empathy in action. It's a driving force that not only acknowledges another's pain or struggle but also seeks to alleviate it. The two together provide a balanced and holistic approach to problem-solving.

A healthcare professional's perspective illuminated this theme poignantly. She said, "You can't treat a patient by looking only at the symptoms. You have to understand their life, their fears, their hopes. That's how you truly heal." This wisdom transcends the realm of medicine. An urban planner echoed a similar sentiment, emphasizing, "When designing public spaces, it's not just about aesthetics or functionality. It's about creating spaces where every individual, regardless of their background, feels welcome and represented."

Several interviewees shared stories where their empathetic approach led to breakthroughs. A mediator in conflict resolution recounted how recognizing the underlying emotions and insecurities of two opposing parties helped find common ground. A teacher spoke of a challenging student who transformed when she understood his home struggles and provided not just academic guidance but emotional support.

In a world that often prioritizes speed, efficiency, and technological advancement, these insights serve as a poignant reminder. The heart of effective problem-solving, regardless of the domain or challenge, is rooted in understanding the human spirit, its vulnerabilities, and its aspirations. When we approach challenges with both empathy and compassion, we don't just find solutions; we touch lives.

Collaboration and Inclusivity

Building Bridges

A powerful message emerged from the interviews we conducted: the profound impact of collaboration and inclusivity. The women we spoke to didn't merely advocate for these values—they actively embodied them in their daily lives, careers, and personal pursuits. By emphasizing the importance of joining hands and interlinking visions, they showcased how unity and diversity can be both a means and an end to advancing positive change.

Building bridges was a recurrent metaphor that came up, symbolizing the creation of connections across varied terrains, be it differences in age, culture, profession, or life experiences. These bridges aren't just structures; they are pathways to mutual understanding, avenues for shared growth, and the embodiment of collective strength. By fostering teamwork and deliberately crafting environments that thrive on diverse input, they set the stage for enriched dialogues and more holistic outcomes.

One tech executive, reflecting on the ethos of her organization, remarked, "In our company, we encourage everyone to speak up. It's the different voices, the unique perspectives, that lead to innovative solutions." Such sentiments were echoed by others in various fields. A medical researcher emphasized the importance of interdisciplinary collaborations, saying, "When we combine expertise from different scientific domains, the results are often groundbreaking." A community organizer spoke about harnessing the collective energy of her local neighborhood: "By pooling our resources and talents, we've been able to address local challenges much more effectively."

These narratives make it clear that collaboration and inclusivity aren't just buzzwords; they're essential strategies for personal and societal advancement. When we prioritize collective effort over individual accomplishment and embrace the full spectrum of human experience, we unlock potentials that are truly limitless.

Research Supporting Holistic Thinking

Modern leadership studies consistently validate the distinct qualities women bring to the table. Grounded in empirical evidence, there's a growing recognition of the holistic and collaborative approach women often employ in leadership roles.

In the landmark study from the "Journal of Applied Psychology," researchers found a rich tapestry of leadership styles and characteristics. At the heart of their findings was the revelation that women leaders often prioritize collaboration. This is not just about working together but creating an atmosphere where ideas are shared freely and every voice is valued.

Empathy stands out as another defining trait. Women leaders, the study suggests, have a heightened ability to understand and relate to the emotions and needs of their colleagues and subordinates. This emotional intelligence allows them to connect deeply, foster trust, and build strong relationships within their teams.

Furthermore, women's leadership is characterized by a broader view of problem-solving. Instead of looking at challenges in isolation, women tend to see the bigger picture. They consider the interconnectedness of issues, understanding that solutions might have ripple effects across various sectors or departments. This holistic perspective nurtures innovation, as it allows for a more comprehensive approach to challenges, ensuring that solutions are both effective and sustainable.

Lastly, an essential aspect highlighted was the focus on social responsibility. Women leaders often intertwine their organizational goals with a sense of purpose and a commitment to the greater good. This aligns with the increasing global emphasis on businesses not just pursuing profits but also contributing positively to society.

This research not only underscores the strengths women bring into leadership roles but also suggests that organizations can benefit immensely by fostering and leveraging these unique qualities. The holistic thinking of women in leadership positions provides a roadmap for innovative, empathetic, and socially responsible governance in any sector.

Your Everyday Wisdom is a Superpower

Throughout the annals of time, there's a certain type of wisdom that often goes unnoticed, a wisdom deeply embedded in daily experiences, interactions, and observations.

It is this everyday wisdom that women, through their unique experiences and perspectives, have honed into a formidable force.

Our interview series illuminated the brilliance of this innate strength, spotlighting the unique lens through which women view and navigate challenges. They approach problems with a fusion of empathy and analytical prowess, discerning not only the hard facts but also the emotional and cultural nuances that interplay in every situation.

This ability to perceive and interpret the world's subtleties, to weave a rich tapestry from individual threads of experience, sets women apart. It's a fusion of intuition and lived experience. It's about recognizing patterns, foreseeing potential challenges, and feeling the emotional currents that flow through personal interactions and larger societal structures.

But more than just a tool for problem-solving, this everyday wisdom is a testament to the power of lived experiences. Every setback faced, every triumph celebrated, every story shared adds to this repository of wisdom. It speaks to the resilience and adaptability of women, who, despite challenges, continuously learn, grow, and evolve.

There's an undeniable alchemy in the way women

transform these daily lessons into strategic insights. In boardrooms, communities, or households, their ability to zoom out and see the myriad of connections and implications is a game-changer. It's akin to viewing a puzzle, not piece by piece, but seeing the beautiful image it's meant to form.

So, to our readers, recognize the magnitude of your everyday wisdom. It's a superpower that has shaped societies, forged connections, and brought about positive change. Value your intuitive insights, your capacity to connect deeply with others, and your unparalleled ability to envision solutions that are both pragmatic and compassionate.

As we move forward in a rapidly changing world, it's this holistic, empathetic, and intuitive approach that will pave the way for a more harmonious and inclusive future. Let's wear our wisdom proudly, and remember, every day offers a new lesson, a new insight, and a new opportunity to make a difference.

Together, We Shape the Future

Insights from Interviews

The culmination of our discussions, the heart of our research, and the resonating theme from hundreds of conversations with inspiring women is crystal clear:

Together, we shape the future. Our interviews have revealed a profound understanding of collaboration, support, and unity. Here's a closer look at the wisdom we've gleaned:

The Power of Support Networks

Human beings are inherently social creatures, yet the weight and significance of genuine, active support networks, especially among women, cannot be overstated. Throughout our discussions, one sentiment resounded like a clarion call: the collective strength that is unleashed when women actively support, mentor, and uplift each other.

Support networks are not just about professional growth; they're sanctuaries of shared experiences, empathy, and mutual respect. For many women, these networks serve as reservoirs of hope during challenging times, as brainstorming hubs to solve shared issues, and as platforms to celebrate each other's successes. There's an unparalleled strength that springs forth when women collectively share wisdom, pool resources, and amplify each other's voices.

Mentorship, a pivotal facet of these support systems, holds a transformative power. Through it, knowledge is passed down, experiences are shared, and newer generations of women are equipped with both the tools and confidence to shatter ceilings. An aspiring entrepreneur we spoke with highlighted, "My mentor didn't just offer advice. She provided me with a roadmap, shared her network, and stood by me during my business's toughest moments."

Beyond formal mentorship, the spontaneous, daily acts of encouragement play a monumental role. A kind word here, a shared resource there, or even a simple acknowledgment of another's achievements can stoke the flames of motivation and persistence. Such acts aren't just about the present moment; they sow seeds for a more collaborative and inclusive future.

The words of a community leader we interviewed beautifully capture this essence: "I wouldn't be where I am today without the support of other women. We create a ladder for each other, and we all climb together." This metaphor of a ladder is poignant, for it suggests that every rung, every step upward, is a collective effort, a result of hands reaching down to pull others up and hands reaching up for guidance.

In the broader societal context, these networks, both formal and informal, don't just empower individual women; they lay the groundwork for systemic change. By fostering environments where women thrive, we are not only nurturing individual dreams but also cultivating communities, industries, and societies that are balanced, equitable, and enriched by diverse voices. As we look to the future, the power of these support networks stands as a beacon, reminding us that when women unite, the possibilities are boundless.

Collective Action for Change

Across the span of history and in the throes of modern society, the narrative remains unchanged: there is immense power in unity. The tales shared with us through our in-depth interviews only serve to amplify this sentiment, shedding light on the transformative nature of collective action, especially when helmed by determined women.

From grassroots movements to global initiatives, women have showcased an unyielding spirit of collaboration. Together, they have tapped into pools of shared resources, skills, and knowledge, often transcending geographical, cultural, and socioeconomic barriers. This synergy of collective minds, working towards a singular goal, has time and again yielded outcomes that are greater than the sum of their parts.

Take, for instance, the mothers lobbying for safer schools, the business leaders pushing for gender-equal boardrooms, or the community volunteers advocating for clean water and sanitation. Each of these endeavors, fueled by the collective determination of women, not only challenges the status quo but paves the way for lasting societal transformation.

Within these collaborative ventures also lies an intricate network of shared stories and lived experiences. These narratives, interwoven with shared struggles and triumphs, become the driving force behind impactful campaigns and initiatives. When women share their stories, they not only find solace in shared experiences but also inspire and galvanize others to join the cause.

Moreover, the digital age has further amplified the scale and scope of collective action. Social media platforms, online communities, and virtual conferences have provided women from every corner of the globe a platform to connect, share, and mobilize. This digital unison has led to global movements, where an issue highlighted in one part of the world finds supporters and allies thousands of miles away.

Echoing the sentiments of an activist we interviewed, she poignantly stated, "When we come together, our voices become a roar. We've seen it time and again – when women unite, we can move mountains." Indeed, this isn't just a metaphorical mountain; it's the formidable barriers of systemic prejudices, age-old biases, and entrenched societal norms.

Collective action among women doesn't just bring about change; it redefines the very landscape of possibilities. As we continue to document these narratives of unity and transformation, one thing becomes abundantly clear: when women collaborate with purpose and passion, the world shifts on its axis, inching closer to a brighter, more equitable future.

Embracing Diversity

Strength in Unity

In a world that often seeks to categorize and box in individuals based on preconceived notions, one of the most uplifting narratives to emerge from our interviews was the unequivocal celebration of diversity. This wasn't just about recognizing differences but actively seeking them out, valuing them, and integrating them into the tapestry of leadership, innovation, and change.

The concept of diversity extends far beyond just the superficial traits that meet the eye. It's about the melding of life stories, cultural backgrounds, personal challenges, individual triumphs, and the myriad experiences that shape one's worldview. Within this vast spectrum of diversity, there lies an enormous reservoir of knowledge, insights, and solutions that can only be accessed when differences are honored and harnessed.

For instance, a young entrepreneur from Asia might approach business challenges differently than her counterpart in Europe, not merely because of her academic qualifications but due to the intricate interplay of her cultural upbringing, societal norms, and personal experiences. When these diverse approaches coalesce, they birth solutions that are more robust, comprehensive, and globally relevant.

Moreover, diverse teams have been proven to be more innovative. With a multitude of perspectives at play, there's a constant cross-pollination of ideas, leading to out-of-the-box thinking and novel solutions. It's akin to looking at a problem through multiple lenses, each offering a unique viewpoint, ensuring no angle is overlooked.

A poignant observation came from a corporate leader we interviewed. She remarked, "Our diverse team is our greatest asset. We learn from each other, and that's what makes us strong." This statement underscores a profound truth: in diversity, there is strength. It's the harmonious blend of varied voices, each singing a different tune, that creates a melody rich in depth and resonance.

Furthermore, embracing diversity extends beyond professional settings. It has profound implications for societal cohesion and progress. When women of diverse backgrounds come together, sharing stories and wisdom, they create a mosaic of experiences. This mosaic, filled with colors and patterns from around the world, serves as a testament to the universal challenges faced by women and the universal strength they showcase in overcoming them.

Diversity isn't just a buzzword or a corporate metric; it's a profound philosophy of inclusivity and unity. As we move forward, it becomes imperative to champion this cause, for in the union of diverse voices, thoughts, and experiences, we find the path to a more enlightened, equitable, and empowered world.

Educating and Inspiring the Next Generation

The resounding chorus from our interviews revealed a shared dedication to educating and inspiring upcoming generations. The women we spoke to were acutely aware of their roles not just as leaders in their fields, but as torchbearers for future trailblazers. Their vision transcended their personal milestones; they viewed their accomplishments and challenges alike as integral to a larger tapestry that weaves through the annals of history, connecting women from eras gone by with those yet to make their mark.

An educator among our interviewees poignantly expressed, "I teach my students that they're part of a beautiful tradition of strong women. I want them to know that they too can change the world." Such sentiments were not isolated.

Another professional from the tech world shared how she makes it a point to spotlight pioneering women in her domain during team meetings, ensuring younger team members realize the shoulders upon which they stand.

This emphasis on lineage and legacy was palpable. Many women spoke about mentorship, emphasizing how mentoring younger professionals was their way of 'paying forward' the guidance and support they received.

They recognized the impact of role models and aimed to be the figures they once looked up to. By instilling confidence, knowledge, and a sense of belonging in younger minds, these women actively contribute to shaping a future that is not only brighter but also cognizant of the rich heritage of resilience and achievement from which it has emerged.

Research and Literature Supporting Collective Impact

The findings from our extensive interviews with nearly 200 men and women beautifully synchronize with existing research on the significance of collective impact in leadership and empowerment.

Elissa Shevinsky's "Lean Out" stands out as a key literary piece in this domain, shedding light on similar themes that echoed throughout our conversations.

Shevinsky masterfully highlights the vital role of women's networks in shaping professional growth and fostering environments conducive to collaboration and trust. This mirrors the sentiments we frequently encountered in our interviews. Many of our respondents voiced the transformative experiences they had within their professional and personal networks.

These networks weren't mere spaces for professional liaising; they emerged as crucibles of inspiration, mentorship, and collective ambition. Similarly, our interviewees frequently underscored the profound influence of community-building in their journeys. They shared stories of camaraderie, of shared goals propelling shared successes, and the unmatched energy of communities united in purpose.

Shevinsky's assertion that such communities can be formidable drivers of social change resonated deeply with our findings. Many of our interview participants spoke of the ripples they observed or catalyzed when women and men leaned into their communities.

The synergy between individual aspirations and collective support, as articulated in "Lean Out", finds parallel narratives in the stories we've documented. It's evident that when people come together with intention and purpose, they don't merely elevate themselves; they create pathways for broader societal elevation, demonstrating the immense power and potential of collective impact.

Our Shared Journey

The narratives shared throughout our interviews provide striking evidence of women's profound ability to influence and inspire.

As mentors, advocates, innovators, and change-makers, our collective strength is undeniable. We don't just overcome obstacles; we redefine the landscape and redraw boundaries for the generations to come.

Diving deep into the digital realm, we were heartened by the immense feedback we received from men and women alike.

Our online interactions, whether through casual discussions, polls, or direct exchanges, reinforced a vital lesson: when women band together, fortified by shared objectives and mutual respect, barriers fade away. This resonating unity transcends divisiveness, underscoring the potential of what we can accomplish in solidarity.

Here are the voices that resonated with this collective spirit:

"Don't listen to the whispers (the inner voice of uncertainty). YOU ARE THE WOMAN FOR THE JOB! Give yourself grace and make sure that you take time daily to reflect on your goodness and all you accomplished. Keep a yearly journal of everything that you do as you add purpose to your career. Journal the journey so that at the end of the year you can reflect on how far you've come and also what it took for you to get there. It helps you to remember your start vs. your finish. It strengthens your 'I CAN' muscles." - *Gladese Cleaves, Commercial Marketing Development Specialist.*

"You might commit mistakes because of inexperience, but don't let anyone tell you that the reason is because you are a woman. Learn from it and move forward." - *Patricia Bona, Vice President, Essence Corporation.*

"View challenges as opportunities to learn and grow. Embrace the reality that nothing in the plan you make for yourself may happen the way you anticipated and that's okay, there's no need to stress. There will be beautiful discoveries to be made on the way that may take you far off track and there are wonderful futures down those paths too." - *Sabwili Mpoyana, Registered Nutritionist/Researcher.*

"The most important thing that we can teach young girls is that their perspective, experiences, and voice are important and powerful to effect change." - *Elizabeth Church, PhD, Director of Science Programs.*

"Embrace your uniqueness and let your authentic voice shine. In a dynamic and evolving landscape, your diverse perspectives and innovative ideas are invaluable assets. Don't be afraid to assert yourself, seize opportunities, and cultivate strong networks. Remember, your presence in the business world is a catalyst for positive change. Believe in your capabilities, keep learning, and stay resilient - you have the power to shape the future you envision." - *Jackie Abbott, Principle in the professional training and coaching industry.*

"Stay authentic to who you are, do not let your environment change you." - *Jessica Marquez, Public Administrative Professional in the non-profit sector.*

In chronicling these shared experiences, we are not only highlighting individual triumphs but spotlighting a wider movement of sisterhood and collaboration. It's a tribute to every woman who has dared to dream, to challenge, and to reshape the world in her unique way.

Dear readers, as we navigate the chapters of our own stories, let's remain steadfast in our commitment to one another, recognizing that our strength is magnified when we stand united. The future isn't something we merely wait for; it's something we actively craft with our actions, beliefs, and aspirations.

It's time we rise, side by side, echoing a resounding message for all to hear: when we come together with compassion, purpose, and tenacity, we are not just influential. We are transformative. The horizon ahead is not just bright; it's ours to shape. Let's forge ahead, for in unity, we find not just strength, but boundless potential.

Key Truths to Empower the Future

- Gender equality is not a destination, but a journey that requires consistent effort, courage, and resilience.
- We stand on the shoulders of women who have led before us, and it's our responsibility to lift as we rise.
- Leadership shows up in everyday moments, in how we support and inspire others.
- We are stronger together, and our collective action can bring about significant change.
- Personal growth and self-belief are integral to leadership. We must own our power and capabilities.
- Each of us has a role in paving the way for future generations of women leaders.

- Let's celebrate the progress we've made while continually pushing for a more equitable future.
- You are amazing!

ABOUT THE AUTHORS

DR. JOLENE CHURCH

Dr. Jolene Church is an accomplished author, seasoned public speaker, and visionary leader in the realms of leadership development and organizational transformation. "Leading the Charge for Change: Women Inspiring Leadership" is her 8th publication, a guidebook meticulously crafted to empower young women by spotlighting the lessons gleaned from the experiences of women interviewed globally.

As the founder and CEO of the Coach Certification Institute, she is responsible for training and certifying some of the industry's finest life and business coaches. Additionally, at the helm of DJC Coaching, Consulting, and Training, Dr. Church masterfully guides organizations in crafting transformational business strategies, fortifying their growth trajectory, and nurturing thriving cultures.

Her academic prowess is evident from her Doctorate of Management in Organizational Leadership. She has not only created innovative curriculum for prominent university graduate programs but also illuminated classrooms as a revered professor.

Dr. Church's speaking engagements resonate with profound insights and have graced platforms of globally renowned organizations, including Intel, Google, and the USC Marshall School of Business. Her early career was marked by her distinctive knack for rejuvenating troubled businesses within Wall Street portfolios.

Beyond her professional endeavors, Dr. Church cherishes a vibrant personal life. Married to Steve, they reside in Northern CA, enjoying the company of their three cats: Baby Kitty, Yang, and Ms. Whiskers. Dr. Church is the proud mother of four grown children and is a doting grandmother to seven. Additionally, she warmly refers to Steve's two children and two granddaughters as her "bonus" family.

Whether embarking on international adventures, feeling the thrill of the open road on their Harley Davidson's, or indulging in outdoor activities, Dr. Church and Steve celebrate life's moments, big and small.

DR. ENNETTE MORTON

Dr. Ennette Morton is a higher education administrator, educator, seasoned public speaker, and thought leader on women's leadership. "Leading the Charge for Change: Women Inspiring Leadership" is her first book publication inspired by her dissertation and presentations which focus on women political leadership.

Born with an insatiable thirst for knowledge, Ennette's parents encouraged and supported her quest for education.

This led to her earning a Bachelor's degree in communication arts-public relations, from California Polytechnic University, Pomona, a MBA in business administration from Pepperdine's Graziadio Business School and a Doctorate in organizational leadership from Pepperdine's Graduate School of Education and Psychology.

In addition to her professional activities, Dr. Morton is an active community volunteer and spends time serving her local community as an appointed city commissioner, and participating with statewide organizations that recruit and train women to run for elected office.

Apart from her professional pursuits, Dr Morton enjoys spending time with her husband James, daughter Ashley, parents Enos and Annie, and two black cats, Pepper, and Pinball in Southern California. A self-proclaimed Francophile, she and James also enjoy traveling to Paris and the French countryside.

BIBLIOGRAPHY

"7 ways to empower women and girls. 2023". World Vision. Retrieved from https://www.worldvision.org/gender-equality-news-stories/seven-ways-empower-women-girls

"62% of UK adults experiencing 'imposter syndrome' at work". (2023). Funding Guru Report. Retrieved from https://www.fundingguru.com/blog/national-study-62-of-uk-adults-experiencing-imposter-syndrome-at-work#:~:text=According%20to%20a%20national%20study,in%20the%20past%2012%20months

"American Express Reports state of women-owned businesses report". (2019, September 29). Manufacturing Close-Up. Retrieved from https://www-proquest-com.proxy-ms.researchport.umd.edu/wire-feeds/american-express-reports-state-women-owned/docview/2298973948/se-2?accountid=12557

"An Increasing Number of Women Are Joining Corporate Boards", [According to Pay Governance Report." Business Wire. 2021, December 8. Business Insights Global. http://bi.gale.com/global/article/GALE%7CA685809042?u=uphoenix

Corbett, H. (2022, April 29). How Women Of Color Are Changing What Leadership Looks Like. Forbes. Online. Retrieved from: https://www.forbes.com/sites/hollycorbett/2022/04/29/how-women-of-color-are-changing-what-leadership-looks-like/?sh=4f9d2a6a6

Difficult Conversations: How to Discuss What Matters Most. (2010. by Stone, Douglas, Patton, Bruce and Heen, Sheila. Penguin Books.

Global Entrepreneurship Monitor (GEM). (2020). Global Entrepreneurship Monitor 2019/2020 Global Report. REtrieved from https://www.gemconsortium.org/report/gem-2019-2020-global-report

Kaprino, K. (2020, October, 22). Forbes. Impostor Syndrome Prevalence In Professional Women And How To Overcome It. Forbes Online. Retrieved from https://www.forbes.com/sites/kathycaprino/2020/10/22/impostor-syndrome-prevalence-in-professional-women-face-and-how-to-overcome-it/?sh=6337c25273cb

Krishnakumar, S., Houghton, J. D., Neck, C. P., & Ellison, C. N. (2015). The "good" and the "bad" of spiritual leadership. *Journal of Management, Spirituality & Religion*, *12*(1), 17-37.

KPMG. (2020, October). Advancing the Future of Women in Business. kpmg2020_WPGAC_study_AK.indd. Retrieved from https://womensleadership.kpmg.us/summit/kpmg-womens-leadership-report-2020.html

Labor Force Statistics from the Current Population Survey. (n.d.). U.S. Bureau of Labor Statistics. Retrieved from: https://www.bls.gov/cps/cpsaat18.htm

Morton, E. Y., "Leadership traits and characteristics of elected California women political leaders" (2013). *Theses and Dissertations*. 338. https://digitalcommons.pepperdine.edu/etd/338

Never Split the Difference: Negotiating As If Your Life Depended On It. (2017).

Voss, Chris. Voss/Raz.

Nice Girls Don't Get the Corner Office. (2018). Frankel, Lois P. Boekerij.

Nurlasera, M. (2019, March). Exploring theory of spiritual leadership: constructing a model. In *16th International Symposium on Management (INSYMA 2019)* (pp. 91-94). Atlantis Press.

Pew Research, 2019. https://www.pewresearch.org/social-trends/2019/01/17/generation-z-looks-a-lot-like-millennials-on-key-social-and-political-issues/

The Confidence Code. (2018). Kay, Katty & Shipman, Claire. Harper Business

Wardell, M.J. (2020). Twice as good. Morgan James. www.MorganJamesPublishing.com

What is Spiritual Leadership? (n.d.) International Institute for Spiritual Leadership. Retrieved from: https://iispiritualleadership.com/spiritual-leadership/

Women in the workforce: Statistics for women in construction. (n.d.) National Association for Women in Construction. Retrieved from https://nawic.org/about-nawic/statistics/

Zheng, W., Ronit, K., & Meister, A. (2018, Nov. 28). How women manage the gendered norms of leadership. Harvard Business Review.